Longing for Arcadia

MEMOIRS OF AN ANARCHO-CYNICALIST
ANTHROPOLOGIST

HAROLD B. BARCLAY

Note for Librarians: a cataloguing record for this book that includes Dewey Decimal Classification and US Library of Congress numbers is available from the Library and Archives of Canada. The complete cataloguing record can be obtained from their online database at: www.collectionscanada.ca/amicus/index-e.html
ISBN 1-4120-5679-9
Printed in Victoria, BC, Canada

Printed on paper with minimum 30% recycled fibre.
Trafford's print shop runs on "green energy" from solar, wind and other environmentally-friendly power sources.

TRAFFORD

Offices in Canada, USA, Ireland and UK
This book was published *on-demand* in cooperation with Trafford Publishing. On-demand publishing is a unique process and service of making a book available for retail sale to the public taking advantage of on-demand manufacturing and Internet marketing. On-demand publishing includes promotions, retail sales, manufacturing, order fulfilment, accounting and collecting royalties on behalf of the author.

Book sales for North America and international:
Trafford Publishing, 6E–2333 Government St.,
Victoria, BC V8T 4P4 CANADA
phone 250 383 6864 (toll-free 1 888 232 4444)
fax 250 383 6804; email to orders@trafford.com
Book sales in Europe:
Trafford Publishing (UK) Ltd., Enterprise House, Wistaston Road Business Centre,
Wistaston Road, Crewe, Cheshire CW2 7RP UNITED KINGDOM
phone 01270 251 396 (local rate 0845 230 9601)
facsimile 01270 254 983; orders.uk@trafford.com
Order online at:
trafford.com/05-0577
10 9 8 7 6 5 4 3

Harold Barclay & Coral
1980

Contents

Preface

This Preface is primarily to explain the meaning of the neologism, anarcho-cynicalist, which appears in the subtitle of this book. It may perplex many readers.

Anarcho refers to the social-political theory of anarchism which holds that the central problem of human society is the problem of power as domination and that the main centre of domination is in the state and government while other forms of domination are to be found in the patriarchal family, in religion, and in predatory economies. Anarchism advocates an end to the various forms of domination. It favors a mutualist society, one based upon mutual aid and voluntary cooperation. It is not the advocacy of chaos, but rather of a radically decentralized, acephalous, kind of society.

Cynicalist refers to cynicism, a rather vague and quite varied philosophical position originating in ancient Greece where it was associated with a criticism of and attack on the basic institutions and values of human society and a questioning of human motives. The Cynic Diogenes claimed to be a citizen of the world and was accused of defacing the currency in addition to other "indecent" acts. The Cynics had some congruence with anarchism. Early Cynics were also noted as advocates of a return to nature and in this respect resemble more closely the current movement for primitivist and anti-civilization anarchism, a position which I find rather difficult to agree with.(1) John Dominic Crossan, in "The Historical Jesus," considered Jesus to be a Semitic Cynic. In recent times the term cynical has come largely to refer to a distrust of human motives and a sour view of humans in general. I am not certain that I bear all the credentials of a cynic, but I use it here as criticism of human institutions. More importantly, it refers to my view that the ideal free society is most unlikely. I have grave doubts that humans will ever extricate themselves from the morass which they have created for themselves, but that despite the horrendous odds against it, despite it being essentially hopeless, we are obligated to continue the fight for freedom and the right. One may note that anarcho-cynicalist is also a play on anarcho-syndicalist, one particular anarchist approach which emphasizes workers control and ownership of industry through union organization November, 2004.

(1) On Cynicism see R. Bracht Branham and Marie-Odile Goulet-Caze (eds.) The Cynics: The Cynic Movement in Antiquity and its Legacy (University of California Press, 1996.)

CHAPTER I
In The Beginning

It was always my feeling that to write one's memoirs and expect anyone else to read them was both an arrogant and silly notion. Now I have been asked by a couple of people to write such a piece allegedly because I have had an interesting life and one which is nearly over. Besides, when one is in his eightieth year reminiscing on one's past becomes an ever increasing activity and attraction. It further provides something to do and to occupy one's mind. Perhaps some of the material could even prove of interest and helpful to others. Some one may read these words and say "Well. now, I thought I was the only one who felt that way, but now I see I am not alone." Thus, with some considerable reservation I here proceed with this venture. I will guarantee any reader, however, that it will not even approach the 950 odd pages of Bill Clinton's monster autobiography. That is, I hope to avoid all verbal diarrhea.

How many people's lives are essentially an answer to their parents? Everyone's life is highly

1

colored by his own parents, at least mine has been. In retrospect I suppose I have devoted a good part of my energy, attempting to deal with my mother and father, seeking to answer them, attempting to divorce myself from them.

My father was a descendant of United Empire Loyalists who settled the rocky shores of Shelburne, Nova Scotia on the invitation of George III (not to be confused with the present King George III, Bush). My father, who lived to be 97 years old, was born in Jordan Falls, Shelburne County, Nova Scotia. He went through the eighth grade in school, the youngest of ten children. Two of these died in infancy; four others died before they were 65, the oldest and the youngest living in to their nineties. As a youngster my father, after whom I was named, spent each summer in his bare feet in order to save shoe leather and was given bread and black molasses as a special treat. Coming from a Baptist family, he was baptized by total immersion in the Jordan River (that is the Jordan of Nova Scotia). At sixteen he became part of the flood of "Down Easters" or Maritimers who moved to the United States, landing in Boston in 1909. He followed his sisters and resided in a rooming house in Auburndale, Massachusetts eventually engaging in automotive repair work.

It was at this rooming house that he met my mother who lived on a small farm in nearby Weston, but spent most of her winters in Auburndale so that she could more easily commute to Boston by train where she attended Sargent School of Physical Education - later to become part of Boston University.

With the US entry into World War I my father readily volunteered to join the army remaining with it until 1919, achieving the rank of corporal as well as his US citizenship.

Following the war he pursued again his occupation of automotive repair, now specializing in auto electrical systems. He spent, I believe, at least, 37 years employed by the same company in Boston.

In 1922 he married my mother after, it appears, a courtship of about ten years and one carried on, I would gather, according to the strict rules of Victorian puritanism. Perhaps I should explain that it seems quite likely that the reason for such a prolonged courtship was the belief born of that Nova Scotian concern for financial security that one should not enter into marriage without some accumulation of savings which could go towards the purchase of a house. On marriage the first major thing they did do was to buy a house in the Boston suburb of Newton-ville where my father could easily take the commuter train every day into Cottage Farm station on the edge of Boston.

As I have intimated my father was not an educated man. I still remember him reading the newspaper with his lips moving to pronounce every printed word. He was also a very conservative man who believed thoroughly in the established order of things - a thorough Victorian with "proper" behaviour to all women, extreme annoyance at any profanity, a teetotaler and one who once as a boy smoked a cigar. He had a strong distaste for any drama, whether on radio, TV or movie, becoming extremely distraught at any conflicts or expressions of sexuality - upright, honest and presumably quiet in every regard. He was rather reticent, not having much to say. I recall my mother coaxing him by suggesting subjects he could talk about when they had company. I think he acquired the reputation of one who was most polite and considerate. However, I soon detected that behind that presumption of quiet, behind the face or mask, was one readily angered, one who seethed with suppressed anger. I also suspect that he often did not have a very high opinion of himself. He sometimes said that he was just a grease monkey.

Possibly a good part of this problem could be my mother's dominant personality. More often than not she seemed to rule the roost and aimed for a more elegant and elevated position in life. When my father died my mother had to fill out a form in which she was asked his occupation. While it should have been auto mechanic, she wrote engineer. She also wrote his education as grade twelve when it was eight. I think she no doubt felt she was telling the truth.

Like many Nova Scotians and New Englanders my father was an inveterate tinkerer. His refuge was in the cellar at his workbench where he did woodworking and repaired our electrical gadgets. He made one invention which was patented. It was called the Barclay Puller, a device for holding an armature for rewinding. Indeed, my mother once thought it would be a great idea if I became a traveling salesman for it.

My mother was born in Weston, Massachusetts, once a small farming community. With the extension of rail service it became home to more well to do businessmen of Boston. She was one of four children of an English father and Nova Scotian mother. Her father operated a small farm raising vegetables, fruit and a few pigs. I believe my mother graduated from Sargent School in 1914, after which she taught in private schools for girls, first in Pennsylvania and then in North Carolina. Once she was married she remained a home maker for the rest of her life except for a few years during World War II when she worked as a sales clerk in a Waltham department store. My mother was what I would have to call a hardnosed individual ever concerned with the dollar and with saving. She was taught well by her Nova Scotian mother on the subject of thrift. Even when my mother was 99 years old and had invested savings of over half million dollars she was greatly concerned about the (to her) real possibility of ending up in the poor house. Along with this was a most uncharitable outlook. I doubt that she ever gave more than a few dollars to any charity. For her the unemployed were just lazy. They could get a job if they wanted to. One should always work even if the income from such labour was much less than that which would come from unemployment insurance or welfare. I am sure that Marx's concept of surplus value or the exploitation of labour by capitalists would be utterly beyond her. She opposed any social security system, although gladly accepted social security cheques when they came to her. She favored the prohibition of alcohol and believed that the most superior and useful positions were those in business. The executives of the big corporations were examples of true success in the world. They legitimately earned all their outrageous wealth. Intellectual or academic activities were frivolous, as were those in the arts. The study of philosophy or history was a complete waste of time. Time should be devoted to business - profit making.

In our house my mother was the one who kept all the financial records and made out the income tax forms. When she died her great drive to save and accumulate rebounded upon her and her legatees, since inheritance taxes took a good portion of the whole legacy.

I do not mean to suggest that one's behaviour and beliefs are totally determined by one's relationship with his parents. However, the influence is certainly very strong. I remember so clearly and starkly my mother's presentation of my father to me as some infallible god. "Why don't you act more like your father?" was what I seemed to hear at every turn. It seemed to my child's mind that no one could ever rise to his divine status, particularly me. I was always inferior and incompetent. I disliked my having to go down into the cellar on my mother's orders to stand around with my father while he repaired some lamp or motor. I was supposed to learn from this. "Why can't you fix things and make things like your father?" Those men who are not competent at repairing and making gadgets are really inferior beings. Interestingly enough nothing of this sort was part of my mother's own capability or personal interest. While my father was the most patient of men in mechanical repair, my mother had no patience whatsoever - a trait I suppose I acquired from her.

It is relevant to mention that I was born at a time when certain rather odd child rearing practices were in vogue amongst middle class Americans. When an infant cried he was not to be picked up and cuddled. In fact, it seems that any display of affection was taboo. Eating times were strictly observed. Whether the baby wanted it or not he was fed at 7, 12, 6, etc. and at no other time no matter how loud the infant screamed. Toilet training was also early introduced and the latter was associated with the notion that it was essential to have a full bowel movement once every day. My mother was always concerned about this daily event and if it didn't occur she was eager to rectify the situation. Overall the program was cold, rigid and indifferent.

As I recall except for my Great Aunt Lillie and Aunt Marion I was never embraced or hugged by any of my relatives. My sister and I both used to kiss our parents before going to bed at night, but it was a rather perfunctory act and stopped by the time we were eleven or twelve. After that the most contact I ever had with my father was a handshake and that only when we hadn't seen each other for a prolonged period. He was always distant and uncommunicative. With my mother it was a slight peck on the cheek or modest hug if I hadn't seen her for some time.

My experience with corporal punishment from my parents was, however, somewhat different. My father actually only physically punished me on one occasion when I was being mean to a girl friend of my sister who was visiting our house. When I misbehaved or got into an argument with my parents my father sat in his chair repeatedly clearing his throat. You could tell he was seething inside - and that along with the throat clearing annoyed me. It was my mother who kept a strap in the kitchen table drawer and actually used it on me on a few occasions. There were a couple of times at least when she washed my mouth out with soap for some wrong doing. I do not recall that my sister was ever punished in these humiliating fashions.

In later years when I had two children of my own, I did slap my son on his bottom on two occasions and once when my daughter was small I picked her up and threw her on her bed. While these actions were all generated by my anger at their behavior and loss of temper, I have actually forgotten the reason for them. Corporal punishment does not accomplish anything except to provide a means for the discharge of pent up anger on the part of the administrator. And this may be followed by feelings of guilt.

My parents, particularly my mother, sought to instill in me a desire for the life of business, an interest in mechanics, a respect for the military and acceptance of mainline Protestant Christianity. All of this I rejected. Clearly I do not claim that my reaction and how I reacted was only an emotional response, although certainly that is of major importance. My beliefs are a product of logical analysis just as much or more so than as a protest against my parents. In any case, as my father was a veteran of World War I, I was a conscientious objector in World War II.

As my parents were rock ribbed Republicans, I was first a socialist and then an anarchist. My mother was a physical education teacher; I hated sports. My father was an electrician and woodworker; I hated mechanics and carpentry. My mother was an Episcopalian and my father a Baptist. I, by age twelve, rejected especially the Episcopalian ritualistic falderal. I was attracted to Unitarians and soon to the Society of Friends. Over my life time I have probably consumed the equivalent of several barrels of antacids!

From my parents, however, I learned the bad habit of an unnecessary dependency, of going to my mother when things went wrong. But I also learned a solid respect for the idea of individual responsibility, a concern for good health and for thrift. A good part of my love for books also is no doubt attributable to my mother. She used to read to me when I was ill and during summer vacation she encouraged me to read some of the "classical." works. My father used to read Peter Cottontail stories from the newspaper to my sister and me. While I acquired an affection for books I was not particularly interested in reading unusual as this may seem. This is because I do not believe that I was ever taught in school how to read correctly.

For one thing I have always been a particularly slow reader. In elementary school and junior high school I avoided reading as much as possible and resisted my mother's urgings to read. It was only when I became older that I actually began to read many books. My parents also taught me in a reverse way - that is, they intended to teach me respect for authority and tradition - but what I learned from this was reaction to it all. I increasingly questioned authority and began to be more skeptical of most things. And I learned, despite them, to have an abiding interest in the welfare of humankind. I could not see the poor as just lazy or black people as somehow inferior.

Despite the criticism I have made here about my mother and father, it must be acknowledged that they tolerated my eventual association with the socialists, my conscientious objection and other rebellious ways. "All of this is just youthful nonsense. He'll grow out of it." Now, in my old age I can see that I clearly overreacted to their discipline. It is likely that their main shortcoming was that they never seemed to demonstrate any love for me and, also, that in my presence my mother seemed to elevate my father to divine status and reduce me to a nonentity. At the same time she encouraged increasing dependence upon her. Rather than some purely Freudian Oedipal sexual situation it was a matter of self respect and, in the broad sense, power for I was being made impotent. Indeed, this is where Freud erred. As Malinowski and others later made clear the family contest is one of power. , although sex may sometimes be involved.

I was born on January 3, 1924 at the Newton hospital, the son of Harold Glenburn (he was called Glen and wrote his name as H. Glen or H. Glenburn) and Mabel Helena Barton Barclay. A little more than a year later my sister, Frances, came on the scene. I actually do not remember too much about our relationship. I was never very close to her and after age seventeen we had only very limited and occasional contact. Of what I do recall is not the happiest for they concern episodes when I seem to have been responsible for some wrong doing in connection with her. For example, there was the time we were out in the garage and I had a pair of scissors and attempted to cut her hair. But I recollect that when we were in high school we would sometimes have pleasant conversations after going to bed at night. We each had bedrooms across the hall from one another.

It has been argued that the eldest child in a family is invariably the more conservative while the middle and younger children are more radical or at least more independent minded. However, in my case the reverse is true. My sister, younger than me, is a very conservative supporter of the status quo - which has been a major factor in my estrangement from her. I have also noted that my case is not peculiar. I do not know what empirical evidence actual supports this notion but my anecdotal evidence shows the contrary. One thing that seems not to be considered in this hypothesis is the sex of the people involved. I would suggest that, given our cultural milieu, it is easier for a child if it is female and that it is she who is more likely to be conservative. It has also been argued that women in general are more conservative because, as those primarily responsible for the domestic realm, they have a more vested interest in its conservation and in tradition. On the other hand, in the recent election in the United States men were more often supporters of the reactionary Bush than were women. Perhaps, though, this may not be entirely related to the issue of conservatism. Women may be more disposed to protecting their rights to abortion, more in favor of gun control and social welfare, and less militarist - all features which would deter one from supporting Bush.

The first thing I actually remember was a trip to Nova Scotia when I was four years old. Anything before that time is one of total amnesia. I accompanied my father to visit his family. The trip made a deep impression upon me so that I vividly remember much that went on: the overnight boat trip on the Yarmouth out of Boston, the stateroom bunk beds; I brought by cedar stuffed rabbit along. There was the train ride from Yarmouth to Shelburne in which a man passed through the train selling pears; there was Uncle Les who drove an old convertible touring car. He pronounced many "gol darns"and gave me my first lesson in firing a rifle(a 22 caliber). Uncle Lyle welcomed me with open arms, but scared me to death when I saw that he didn't have a right hand - it having been cut off in a sawmill accident. There were the big beds with no springs, the oil lamps and outhouses and the oxen. It was the first and only time I ever saw my father cry. I believe it was because his mother, who was ill with some terminal ailment, did not know him. There may have been several years since he had been home.

One of my early favorite toys was a car my father

made for me out of pieces of metal. I could sit in the seat and move the vehicle with peddles. Influenced by my father I took an early, albeit not long lasting, interest in automobiles. I used to like going with him to the annual auto show, especially visiting the Mack truck salesroom. I was also early put to sharing household tasks such as mowing the lawn in summer and shoveling snow in winter. My sister and I also washed and dried dishes after supper. I believe that, while I might have fussed about these activities at the time, this sharing in these duties is most worthwhile for child training especially in teaching responsibility and mutual aid.

Deeply impressed upon my memory was the time that I had my tonsils and adenoids removed long ago in 1930. The surgeon and our local general practitioner came to the house and I laid on the living room couch while being administered a cone of ether. I can smell it to this day and feel the horrible sensation of suffocation. Later I learned that once I had passed out, I was carried to the kitchen table where the operation was performed. I awoke with a very sore throat.

Another early experience which I have remembered most vividly occurred when I was about five. I threw a stone at a three year old neighbor of ours - a chubby little girl for whom I had developed a strong distaste. The rock struck her forehead. My mother made me go to her house and apologize to her parents and promise I would never do such a thing again. Two or three years later I was sent off with my sister to dancing lessons and was paired up with another chubby little girl. When I had to hold her hands I recall attempting to squeeze them hoping to hurt her. As near as I can determine today these reactions were most likely a disguised expression of hostility to my own sister. I did not care for these lessons. Luckily I believe they didn't last long because the teacher discontinued them. At least during this time in the 1930's it was common for middle class families to send their children to both dancing and piano lessons. The latter I was exposed to for a couple of years, but only a few years later I had forgotten everything I had ever learned about a piano.

About age seven or eight my mother decided that it would be good for me to go to summer camp. I was not at all enthusiastic. Therefore, she sought to coax me to go by offering me a set of five hundred foreign stamps. I had recently begun to collect stamps - an activity I pursued until entering high school when

I sold the collection for three or four dollars. The stamp buyer was willing to pay that amount because there was apparently one stamp he really wanted. I accepted my mother's offer (bribe?) of the stamps and that summer packed off to the camp. There was little about the experience that I enjoyed. I was extremely lonesome, so much so that when after the first week my parents visited me I broke down in great tears. Except for the opportunity to swim I was uninterested in the activities of the camp and indeed they often provoked in me considerable anxiety. The camp directors had set aside one night each week in which everyone gathered and any camper could challenge another to a boxing match. These occasions were most unpleasant for me since I was afraid of being challenged, although no one ever did.

At one time I had a great desire to have an electric train and before Christmas let it be known that that is what I would really like as a present. Christmas morning came and my sister and I came down to the fireplace where our presents would be, but there was no train. I walked all around the dining room table beside the fireplace searching without success. Next year I received the train which I ran regularly for a few months before becoming bored with it. Another

Christmas I was given a chemistry set which I greatly enjoyed. I always liked Christmas presents from an aunt and uncle, Mildred and Rexford Davis. He taught English at Rutgers University and, thus, had an interest in books. They gave me a book each year. My mother was always reluctant to buy any books for me. Books were not things one needed to own. You can always go to the public library and borrow a book for nothing was a view she adhered to throughout her life. I am sure this attitude is one which would please all professional writers.

I did manage, eventually, to acquire some books. My great uncle, James Pirie, by occupation a farm manager, had been sort of a bookophile and, consequently, was one relative I always wished I had been able to know. He died from diabetes about a month or so before insulin was discovered and left editions of Darwin's and Spencer's works along with a complete set of the Encyclopaedia Brittanica, a 1903 edition. They had been stored since his death in my Aunt Marion's attic and I now acquired them. I often tried to read Encyclopaedia articles and had no little trouble trying to understand them. Once in desperation I inquired of my mother for help but she ridiculed my queries. Perhaps she didn't understand the material any more than I did, but this experience made me quite secretive about my reading and writing.

Until I was thirteen I was forced to go to Sunday School at the local Episcopal church. I don't remember much of this except for the last year I attended. The Sunday School classes were divided by sex and approximate age and I was in a group of eight other boys, a class which was considered so difficult to handle that the minister had to take over. I didn't much enjoy it. For one thing all eight of us were supposed to sit in one pew which meant that one student was always squeezed into an awkward position. That one student was always me. At this time I was beginning to have an interest in various religious and philosophical problems. Consequently, I invariably used the Sunday School period to ask the minister various questions and on occasion attempt to argue with him. This exchange only pleased the other boys in the class because it meant that they only had to sit back and avoid dealing with the lesson for that day. Soon it came to be that before a class started they would eagerly urge me to engage the minister in argument.

Finally, I so vigorously protested having to attend

this school that my mother allowed me to leave it on condition that I go to regular church services. She even agreed that the church did not have to be the Episcopal and that maybe I didn't have to attend every Sunday. Thus, I began attending with my mother the local Congregational and the Unitarian churches, both of which I found reasonably acceptable. Once and a while we would go somewhere else, even one time to the Swedenborgian Church. Compulsory church ended when I left home to attend Stockbridge Agricultural School in Amherst where I took up with the Society of Friends (Quakers). Well before this, however, I had invented my own sect, the Humanitarian Society, which, although theistic, stressed issues of human relations. I lost interest in it when I discovered the Quakers.

About the same time that I invented the Humanitarian Society I invented my own political party, the Union People's Party. This actually entailed a very silly idea. I proposed to have a totally centralized state where all authority and decisions were to made in Washington. State, county, and town administrations were to be abolished as autonomous entitles. Once I mentioned to my father my idea of "Unionism" to which he replied that we already have far too many 'isms'. Within a year I had given this idea up in favor of a Progressive People's Party which had a more sensible program. I had become especially interested in the cooperative movement and even wrote my first letter to the editor of the "Boston Traveler" which appeared in the October 29, 1937 issue on the subject. A year later I wrote a second letter to the same newspaper offering a program for prosperity. Actually, it was the program I had concocted for the Progressive People's Party. It advocated "processing, distribution and marketing of all farm products by the cooperative movement. A Balanced budget maintained by the pay as you go policy. A voluntary crop control program, an ever normal granary plan and a soil conservation act for the benefit of the farmers, a bank to be organized where tenant farmers may borrow money without interest so as to buy their own farms, employment exchanges and unemployment insurance to abolish unemployment. Work relief for all those unemployed persons who are capable.

"Workers control and ownership of industry, thus destroying capitalistic as well as government control of industry. The right to strike peaceably and to practice collective bargaining. A federal housing program and wages and hours act. Compulsory social security for all Americans, excluding the wealthy, over 60 years of age in monthly allowances of $100 to be spent within the month. Abolition of monopolies and holding companies.

"A drastic reduction in arms, peace to be maintained under a policy of absolute neutrality in all foreign wars and scraps. War to be declared only in the case of invasion of the United States itself and no American troops, warships and war planes, of any kind, number or for any militaristic reason shall ever leave the United States or go beyond a 200-mile limit at sea.

"Government control of liquor on a non-prohibitive basis and similar to that program used in Finland today."

The above program reflects major issues of the day as well as my own interests in agriculture. It, of course, also entails a few contradictions. For example, if workers are to control and own industry why do you need to have a provision about strikes and collective bargaining or one about monopolies and holding companies? Well, I was fourteen years old when I wrote it.

One of the more enjoyable experiences of childhood was our family Thanksgiving and Christmas dinners. Of course, Thanksgiving was not as great an occasion as Christmas since the latter entailed a decorated tree and gifts. On both occasions usually fourteen or fifteen people assembled, all relatives through my mother. My aunt Marion and my mother took turns having these affairs and I alway enjoyed it most when we could go to Aunt Marion's. I always thought she had a better tree with far better decorations. She lived in the 'rurban' fringe of Boston where we could go for country walks after the heavy dinner. The atmosphere at her house seemed always freer and happier. Marion was the oldest of my mother's siblings and was always easy going, extroverted and loving.

For each holiday there were two turkeys. At one end of the table was the turkey with oyster dressing and at the other one with plain. We had mashed potatoes, squash and creamed onions and cranberry sauce. Eventually, I became the one to peel most of the onions because I didn't cry so much from the onion juice. There were several desserts including home made plum pudding with hard sauce and lemon sauce, squash and mince pies and sponge cake.

After dinner my father, Uncle Ed and Uncle Rex

sat around talking about cars and also about politics. Ed and my father were Republicans and Rex was a Democrat and compelled to defend the Roosevelt New Deal. My Grandfather and Uncle Walter more often fell asleep in a chair. On Christmas afternoons we eventually settled around to distribute the Christmas gifts. It was always difficult to have to wait so long for the gifts since my sister and I unpacked Christmas stockings and presents from our mother and father in the morning, but received all the other presents from other relatives in the late afternoon. Incidentally, I do not recall any belief in Santa Claus; I certainly had given up that idea by the time I was five if not before.

I accompanied my parents and sister on various trips including Niagara Falls, Washington, D. C. and a major expedition to the Gaspe Peninsula in Quebec and the Maritime provinces. In Quebec most everyone still went around in horse and buggy. The line villages had small houses for the size of the families inhabiting them. From passing the houses on the road it always appeared that the most important part of the house was the huge and well polished kitchen stove. Of course, each village had its enormous church and the biggest house was always that for the priest many of whom seemed to fit the stereotype: a rather fat man dressed in black cassock and smoking a cigar.

Much of New Brunswick which we passed through from Quebec seemed like the frontier and the wilderness with isolated small, sometimes log, houses with small clearings having at best a potato patch. I will not forget Moncton, New Brunswick where we stayed in over night cabins - the ancestor of the motel - and my sister and I became deathly ill presumably from the extremely hard water in the vicinity. My father's relatives in Nova Scotia still had oil lamps, outhouses, and outdoor wells for water and my uncle had a yoke of oxen which he used especially in winter for hauling logs.

A couple of summer vacations, each of a week or so duration, were spent on Cape Cod in a rented cottage. This region may have been attractive when Henry David Thoreau traveled through it 150 years ago, but it is now so densely populated and so full of honky tonk that it is not that pleasant a place.

Generally speaking, childhood is not the happiest of times, and my school days in particular were not the best of days. They were often downright miserable. I was quite upset on being sent to kindergarten and was passed into the second grade on trial. Apparently the problem was difficulty in reading and that seemed to be because of defective eyesight which was corrected by glasses. Beginning at age eleven I commenced having periodic temper tantrums as a consequence of my relations with my parents.

With the exception of social studies and history I did not care much for school. I disliked mathematics and was often kept after school to do long division and large numbers for multiplication which, of course, is hardly conducive to encouraging one to like the subject. Algebra and geometry were difficult for me and my mother spent many hours with me attempting to complete homework assignments in both subjects. She did the same when it came to French lessons. I suppose I have portrayed my mother as a rather flint like individual, but she was eager to protect me ,which obviously increased my dependence upon her. The odd thing is that she would readily break down and cry in situations where I had misbehaved. Two or three times when I was involved in minor disciplinary problems at school (not being respectful to the teacher) my mother on each occasion broke down. She did this on other occasions as well. So maybe there was something soft behind all that apparent hardness, just as with my father there was something hard behind all his outer calm.

English classes had some redeeming features. I enjoyed giving what my fellow students often called "oral talks." Once I gave a talk on Mahatma Gandhi and non-violence. In high school I wrote an essay denouncing compulsory military training. This was about 1939 or 1940 when such issues were being considered and the patriotic baloney was heightened. The teacher put a huge question mark on the top of the page, not giving me any grade. "You don't really believe this do you?" she asked. At the same time I began to have qualms about the making the pledge of allegiance to the flag, although I conformed with tongue in cheek.

I was never interested in or very good at sports. Actually I hated most of them. In school we were exposed from grammar school to high school during the warmer months to baseball which I came to detest above all. We used to be lined up and a couple of the Great Players were made captains and told to select members for a team. I was usually the last one to be picked for any team. When it came time to go to bat I, as much as possible, attempted to avoid my turn.

In fall, the problem was football. I never learned how to throw a football and never learned even the first thing about how the stupid game was played. In the winter when we played volleyball it was easier and there was less anxiety. I never learned ice skating and I later took to a bit of skiing with those old kinds of skis where you thrust your feet through a thong on the ski. My sister and I used to ski down a hill on my grandfather's farm.

Sports were not for me and I detested all those big shot athletes. I still do - it is obscene to pay some moronic basketball player millions of dollars a year while a heart surgeon or an important researcher or creative person gets one tenth or less of that amount.

I went off into my own world. At first I devoted some time to drawing, especially faces. Once in school two or three of us were looking at a book from which I had copied several drawings. As we turned the pages to look at a picture I would say "I drew that," meaning I copied that while the literal minded companions said "You did not"... "I did so"...

More in the world of fantasy I began to create other countries. These were chiefly islands and more often than not rather barren or desert like places.

I have always been interested in such refuges and have spent no little time in investigating and reading about the Falkland Islands, Tristan da Cunha or Iceland. However, I have only visited Iceland and really don't think I would care to live in any of them if only because they seem to be so windy and I hate wind. For my invented lands I drew maps showing mountains and rivers and towns and wrote out tables of population and characteristics of the population. I was particularly interested in agricultural statistics so that I would write out the number of cattle, horses and swine or the amount of land in this or that crop, the number of farms and farm population. I even compiled statistics for religious sects and their distribution.

My real refuge from family and school became my grandfather's farm. Fifty or sixty years ago there were still a few small farms in the "rurban" fringe around the edges of the Boston metropolitan area. My grandfather owned one of these farms - twenty acres of rocks and hills on which he raised mostly sweet corn, tomatoes, squash, strawberries, and apples. He also raised pigs and kept two or three cows. I spent most of my adolescence on the farm.

My grandfather's claim to fame aside from living

to be 94, was that he was likely the first person to establish a roadside vegetable stand in America. In 1900, when automobiles were first appearing among the well to do, he sold his produce from the stone wall by the road to passers by who came out from the Boston suburbs for a Sunday drive.

Grampa was a very conservative farmer as far as tools and machines were concerned. From him I learned to milk, to harness and drive a team, manipulate a walking plow and ride a hay rake. Today when I go to certain museums I see items and implements, now alleged to be antiques, which I learned to use as a boy.

There was a queer kind of wagon on the farm which took some practice to drive. If turned too sharply the front wheels pushed under the body tipping it so that one could easily lose a load. In order to turn safely one had to inscribe a very wide arc. "You're not driving a Ford truck," my grandfather would comment.

One item my grandfather came to sell from his roadside stand (after the First World War it became a small building) was dressed poultry. Thus, on Friday nights I would go out to the hen house with him to pick chickens off the roosts and take them to a small shack where my grandfather chopped their heads off and tossed them into a barrel thickly stained with the dried blood of previous victims. We then doused the bodies in boiling water and plucked the feathers and Grampa then eviscerated them.

On the farm I became acquainted with Ralph Demeo who had already worked for several years on the farm. Ralph was fifteen years older than I was. I came to like him very much and thought of him as a friend, although I was never quite sure that he was only tolerating me because I was the boss's grandson. I joined him in picking vegetables, hoeing weeds, leading the horse while cultivating and in haying. We eventually began to exchange Christmas presents. Once the United States entered the Second World War Ralph left the farm and joined the army. He had been for some time displeased with the place and his employers. I regret that I never saw him again even though after the war was over he returned to the Boston area, to his home in Waltham, only three miles from where I was living.

A ubiquitous problem on the farm was rats. I used to take a hay fork and steal into the grain room in the barn and quickly flip open the cover to the bin and, if lucky, impale a rat amongst the grain.

In summer the corn was cultivated with a one horse cultivator. The horse had to be led to prevent him from nibbling the corn stalks. Of course, a more efficient method would be to muzzle the horse, but perhaps here the Biblical injunction against muzzling one's ox was remembered. All too often my job was to lead the horse which was all right except that at the end of the corn field there was bush and poison ivy. For some inexplicable reason the horse liked the ivy and whenever he could he would take a swipe at it. In time his bit and the corners of his mouth were covered with the juice which inevitably passed on to me, and unlike the horse I was very allergic to poison ivy. It was the bane of my existence. It grew everywhere - around trees, stone walls, across the ground. My arms and legs would be covered with great itching blisters and at the time no one I knew seemed to have any notion about how to treat it. I even had injections which were supposed immunize me against the stuff, but to no avail. Eventually someone recommended calomine lotion which helped a bit.

Learning to plow for me as an adolescent was a great challenge. It could be enjoyable as long as the horses behaved - one keeping in the furrow and one on top so as to keep something of a straight line - and also as long as you didn't hit any big rock. A bad thing about plowing was the rocks. New England is full of rocks and this place had more than its share. When one hits a hidden rock the size of your head with a walking plow it jars the horses; the whole harness shakes. Worst of all the plow handles punch you in the stomach. My furrows were never as straight as an arrow, which is what they were supposed to be.

Haying was as much fun as it was labour intensive. The hay meadows were cut with a two horse mower, raked with a single horse rake, set in cocks by hand and loaded and unloaded by hand. A good stacker knew how to distribute the hay on a wagon so as to take a maximum load which would stay on. A big load of hay on the wagon I mentioned earlier could be hazardous negotiating turns and especially trying to bring it up close to the door of the barn loft.

I sometimes phantasized about driving a team of horses into the midst of Newton High School or sitting back and laughing as the Great Athletes tried to plow a field, milk a cow or make a good hay stack.

The best time of year was between July and October. There were blueberries in the woods which meant blueberry pies. Above everything else there was sweet corn. It was always best in a pale yellow stage and when eaten within fifteen minutes or so of being cooked. The unknowing speak of eating cobs of corn. What you eat is an ear of corn and the cobs are what is left over after eating.

Finally, October was appreciated because it was usually still reasonably warm and dry and the trees a blaze of colour. It was also a time when some interesting things had to be accomplished. At least at that time I thought they were interesting. The corn stalks, which were used for stock feed, had to be cut. I remember the first time I cut the stalks. The job was done with a sickle and I went at it with youthful gusto so that my hands were blistered. I also cut the stalks letting them fall where they may and not placing them in proper piles so they could be easily picked up. The sight of the field strewn with corn stalks did not appeal to my grandfather.

October was also the month to pick squash and the apples. I didn't care much about apple picking. First there was the poison ivy around the base of the trees. Then, I didn't care much about climbing and moving ladders. Apples marked the end of the season. November would be gray, rainy and cold and the entry to winter. By this time on the farm one began to look forward to March and April. The primary activity in winter was to feed the pigs and put hay bedding in their houses. Occasionally, a pig would be slaughtered. I did not appreciate the pig sticking, the poor pig being raised by one leg on a pulley and his throat jabbed with a knife. It was then dumped into hot water and the bristles scraped off. Then the internal organs were removed. The carcass was cut up and my grandfather made sausage and head cheese with miscellaneous parts.

Today this farm no longer exists. Thick bush covers most of what once was and at one corner, where the pig pens used to stand, there is a church. Things change; sometimes not always for the better.

All children seem to become bonded to one or another adult relative. Ideally, in our culture a boy should look to his father, but I did not, for reasons I have already indicated. My mother's father became the alternative. He was born in 1858 in Horton, Gloucestershire, England and immigrated to the United States in the 1870's. His father had been a tenant farmer, part of the Winchcomb estate. While my grandfather had been apprenticed as a butcher, on coming to the US he worked as a farm labourer.

He once told me about one Christmas eve when there was only he and another fellow available on the farm to milk - by hand - one hundred cows. This would require at least four or five hours.

Evenings on the farm I would frequently indulge in long political discussions with my grandfather, He was, of course, a political conservative as well as a stalwart supporter of the British 'Empire. I took exception to most of his ideas, although we tended to agree on agricultural matters. One of the latter I remember concerned pasteurization of milk. The "Rural New Yorker," to which my grandfather subscribed, campaigned against pasteurization and my grandfather, who did not believe in the germ theory of disease, supported this position. At the time I thought that made sense, too.

My grandfather married my grandmother in 1886. She was a Nova Scotia immigrant who was employed as a maid on a wealthy estate outside of Boston where my grandfather also worked. By 1893 he had purchased the small farm in Weston which he named Winchcomb after his English home. He managed the place until the 1940's when he relinquished it to his son, my Uncle Walter, who ran it until his death in 1963.

I never had much to do with my grandmother whom I did not always find that likable. However, her sister, my Great Aunt Lillie, also lived on the farm, having moved there after her husband's death. He was James Pirie whom I mentioned above. I was always very fond of Aunt Lil. We used to talk together and take walks. She was always very kind, easy going, and most sympathetic, perhaps one of the few sympathetic people I knew at this time, although my mother's older sister, Marion, was equally so.

Sometime during the 1920's my grandfather began to raise Cocker Spaniels for sale and when I came to the farm I pretty much took over feeding and care of the dozen or more dogs. I was given a dollar for any puppy that I sold and I became greatly attached to some of the dogs. Cocker Spaniels are supposed to have their tails docked as puppies. Thus, I would go with my grandfather, tie off the little tails and hold the pups while he cut off the tails with his jackknife . I should say a word about that jackknife. Grampa also used it for castrating pigs and once when we were on a fishing trip in Boston Harbor for lunch he took out a cucumber and using that old knife proceeded to cut off slices and offer them to me. I declined them.

Once Grampa gave my sister and me the runt of a litter of puppies. Because the pup was so small and also was a reddish colour my sister thought we should call her Penny. But Penny was only with us for a year when she contracted distemper and died.

I was always jealous of my grandfather's attention and did not like it one bit when he seemed to favour a boy my age who came to work on the farm after school. Nor did I much care for the favoritism he seemed to show to my sister.

As I have mentioned my Uncle Walter took over management of the farm in the 1940's, but even before this time he had assumed the bulk of the operation. I never appreciated him and often used to criticize the way he ran the farm. He did not seem to do much work and appeared to me to maintain a messy and unkempt place. I cannot, however, say that he was not always good to me. When I was twelve or thirteen he often took me with him on trips to nearby Auburndale where he bought me an ice cream cone. During the summer he took me along to a farmers' market at six o'clock in the morning and afterwards I accompanied him to a restaurant for a breakfast of bacon and eggs. I also joined him in taking loads of pigs to the Brighton stockyards. Later I came to realize that I was unfair to Walter. He was essentially the victim of his parents. As a young man Walter wanted to become an accountant or bookkeeper. When he proposed leaving the farm to seek such work, his mother burst into tears and begged him to remain on the farm to help his father and succeed him when he became indigent. Thus, to appease his mother, Walter gave up his own career aims to spend his life on the farm which he never cared for. While Walter never had a difficult or insecure life, like so many others, he didn't exactly get a fair shake in life.

All my experience on the farm and with my grandfather have impressed on me a long lasting and emotional tie to the farm idea. Even today I am most concerned about the status of agriculture and the preservation of the family farm. My nostalgia harks back to a time before the extensive mechanization of agriculture and certainly before the advent of agribusiness. Most modern agriculture is far from that which I experienced - a way of life which has now long since past. Yet, I still continue to be drawn to the farm. It is difficult to appreciate that what exists today is so removed from what I really enjoyed and indeed represents a highly mechanized and business type life that I do not like.

At home in Newtonville there were a couple of neighbor boys that I played with until I was about thirteen after which we lost contact. One thing we used to do was to go to the woods near my house where we built make shift shelters from saplings cut with a jackknife. We sat around a fire and later we picked up cigarette butts from the street, dumped out the tobacco and made little acorn pipes to smoke. We tried cornsilk, too, but that was really hot.

In junior and senior high school I was pretty much a loner. Junior high school was particularly unpleasant. One teacher there decided that everyone was to participate in a checkers competition. He proceeded to rank all thirty of us from number one at the top to number thirty at the bottom as a starting point. He gave me the bottom number so that if I hoped to win I would have work my way up from the bottom to first position.

Everyone else had an advantage over me so I didn't bother to play. I thought school was full of this kind of discriminatory nonsense.

I had numerous "crushes" on "pretty girls" in school and frequently phantasized about them although I never dared approach them. My first crush began in the third grade with Jane Finnell and I seem to have continued with one or another every year through to the end of high school. I can even now remember all their names and what they seemed to look like, but none did I ever dare speak to, although I certainly phantasized a lot about such encounters.

I was seventeen before I ever had the gall to speak to a "pretty girl" and ask her for a date. Jean Smith was the daughter of Nova Scotian immigrants who, as I look back now, were economically quite poor. Her father lost his job hauling heating oil as a result of the Second World War and at sixty years of age and with little education had difficulty finding employment. Jean was in Wayland high school and used to come to Dean Dairy to buy ice cream during the summer when I was working there. It took a considerable amount of goading from fellow employees at the dairy for me to ask her if I could come to see her. It was an infatuation which lasted several months although the relationship persisted for over a year. She was from a strong Baptist family and I suppose one of the frustrating features of the relationship was her adamant insistence that any intimacy would go no further than mere hugging. She would not even permit me to kiss her. We entered into a routine where I would come to visit and we would go for a walk and then return to her house for smooching. Until December 7, 1941 our relationship was, I thought, very good. I could not accept the war which commenced at this time and I also could not accept that Jean would approve of it either. I began to nag and plague her about the subject and that eventually put an end to the affair. In September of the following year while I was living in Amherst, Massachusetts she wrote me a letter stating that she never wanted to see me again.

In 1940 I had joined the Young Peoples Socialist League, youth branch of the Socialist Party. During that year I spent a considerable amount of time campaigning for the presidential candidate, Norman Thomas. I distributed probably thousands of leaflets from door to door and volunteered to work in the party office in Boston doing such things as folding fliers and pamphlets, or writing addresses. By that time the Socialist Party in Massachusetts had dwindled to perhaps a hundred members, a result of a major split in the party over support of Roosevelt's New Deal and later the war issue. I remained in the Socialist Party for six years. In the 1942 election, at eighteen, I gave a speech from the Socialist platform on Boston Common. I criticized the capitalist system and advocated the socialization of the means of production and distribution. I did not agree with what the Socialist Labor Party people called "sewer socialism" which seemed to be popular among members of the Socialist Party. "Sewer socialism" largely ignored the ultimate goals of the party, namely, socialism, and focused on "immediate demands," a long list of reforms of the existing system such as better wages, shorter hours, health and unemployment insurance. I favoured socialism as the one "immediate demand." In this way I agreed with the Socialist Labor Party and the smaller Workers Socialist Party. One article I wrote at this time for the 'internal organ' of the Socialist Party took the party to task for not sticking to 'pure' socialism. Someone from the Socialist Labor Party got hold of the article and published it in their periodical, "The Weekly People," suggesting I should join them.

Sometimes I would go with Howard Penley, state secretary of the Socialist Party, to Sunday night meetings of the Workers Socialist Party. This group later changed its name to World Socialist Party to avoid confusion with Trotskyites such as the Socialist Workers Party. It was also nicknamed the Wisps and was affiliated with the Socialist Party of Great Britain.

Once when I was still under the influence of Spinoza I made a short talk at a Wisp meeting on why a Socialist could believe in god. That is, he could accept the pantheist view as god as the sum total of all things. Mr I. Rabb, who acted as chairman of the meetings and leader of the Wisps responded to my observations. He said Spinoza was a typical bourgeois thinker; why not refer to the sum total of all existence as the phantasmagoria... which made me wonder. The Wisps were a very open group, willing to listen to all arguments. At the same time they were strict Marxists and for Marxists such tolerance was not common. While I sympathized with much of what the Wisps and the SLPers had to say I never bothered to ally myself with either of them. Both groups were so minuscule, ineffective and doctrinaire I thought they could not possibly get anywhere. The Socialist Labor Party also appeared quite authoritarian.

CHAPTER II
Floundering Around

I had graduated from high school and now decided to follow more in my grandfather's footsteps and become a farmer. My interest at the time was in dairy cattle and for a short period during the summer of 1941 I worked on a large dairy farm which had well over one hundred milking head. Most of the cattle were milked with machines, but part of the barn was not equipped for them so the cows had to be milked by hand. It was my job, after helping to clean out the barn in the morning, to milk twelve of them. Every day was largely devoted to haying and evening chores began about 4: 30 and ended by 6: 30. The operators insisted that I work over twelve hours a day six days a week plus four or five hours on Sunday for a small pittance. Therefore I did not remain long at this place and instead spent the rest of the summer dishing out ice cream cones at a dairy. I applied to the Stockbridge School of Agriculture associated with Massachusetts State College in Amherst and in the fall of 1941 I entered their two year program in animal husbandry which led to a diploma. During the year I wrote to Jean about everyday when I could not visit her on holidays.

It has always been hard for me to strike up acquaintances and make friends; it has always been a time of intense anxiety for me to approach strangers and establish friendships. It isn't that I dislike people. My greatest delights have been the good fellowship of a gathering of friends for good food and drink and entertaining and enlightening conversation. At Stockbridge I found a few friends. One was an Amherst College freshman who lived in my rooming house.(Amherst College was also located in the town of Amherst at the opposite end of the town from Massachusetts State). At Amherst he took courses in philosophy and read Spinoza. We spent many evenings in discussion and I became convinced of Spinoza' s pantheism. On my own I began to delve into Kant and Hume and then Hegel. Strangely it never occurred to me at the time that such intellectual endeavours is where I should be devoting my time rather than in dairy cattle.

I don't believe that I understood Kant very well and what I read of Hegel I did not particularly like. It was all so ponderous, dense and absolutist.

Kant ,I eventually learned a few years later , offered in part at least an outlook which fitted in with my views on anthropology and a world outlook. Helpful in this regard was Ernst Cassirer's "Essay on Man."I have, off and on over the years, struggled with Kant's work and important to me is his idea that the mind has a structure through which we perceive the external world as appearances. Our direct encounter is with our mind so that we know the world indirectly only through our mind. Schopenhauer whom I read a few years later and found the easiest of all philosophers to read, had said "The world is my idea."

In the present day while most would not agree with the categories of components attributed by Kant to the structure of the mind I think the idea of a mental structure through which we perceive reality is widely received if not exactly as Kant outlined it. I think that Cassirer adapted Kant to anthropological theory and the concept of culture. A long time cornerstone of anthropology has been the concept of culture - that since birth each of us has been brainwashed with cultural tradition which becomes embedded in our minds so that we see the world through cultural glasses. It is a world of appearances. Even science is not immune to cultural influences.

We can say that humans are immersed in a symbolic world, the symbols being the cornerstone of a culture. This was Cassirer's modification or addition to Kant. For Cassirer humankind is Homo symbolicus. Therefore, we may say that, in addition to a structure of the brain, we eventually have impressed upon us a body of acquired ideas and both of these then focus our view of the world in a specific fashion. The world appears to us as it is because of the filtering of "reality" through both the structure of our brain and the acquired culture.

Noam Chomsky has suggested that somewhere in the human mind is a propensity for language and that all languages a have a broad common structure which is in the mind. Language, as the most important component of culture and as a symbolic system, clearly biases our view of the "real" world.

We might then say, drawing ultimately from Kant, that the mind has a structure, part of which is genetic and part is acquired. The structure as a whole provides a world of appearances and we can never be sure of what some ultimate reality or "nuomena" might be.

I have in the above discussion commenced with my adolescent vague experience of Kant and then presented my understanding of him acquired at a later time. I have also used the word 'mind' and here probably should now clarify, at the present time, what I mean. In Western philosophy there has been much discussion of the so-called body-mind problem. It is interesting that this is an issue which has not much disturbed Asiatic or Eastern philosophy. To simplify the problem I would say that mind is brain plus all the acquired ideas and notions of the individual. The brain interacts with the environment and consequently mind emerges as all that has been acquired being encased in the brain. There is no blank slate as Locke would have it. However, the structure is sufficiently "loose" so that what the individual learns readily directs him in ways which vary from his neighbor.

The claims of such people as Pinker and others that the inherited and genetic structure of the brain almost totally determines human behavior ignores the powerful effect of culture upon the individual. From conception the brain is accumulating information such that each develops a view of the world. But this does not mean that there is no reality outside my idea. We believe there is a "real" world out there partly because so many features of that world are commonly recognized by everyone else. In addition, the results of much modern science support such a view. It is, of course, possible that what we may all agree upon and what science confirms may all be some great illusion. But I would like to doubt that this is really so.

Although there are phenomena which we see in the same way as everyone else, there are other phenomena which would be seen the same as other members of one's own cultural group and not by others. They are culturally determined. There are also some which lend themselves to an interpretation peculiar to a single individual. For one to have several peculiarly individual interpretations may make him a candidate for the lunatic asylum. In a way life is a continual attempt to test our perception of reality against the ultimate reality.

Descartes thought the mind was purely a kind of spiritual entity and that animals were automatons with no minds, but it seems to me that animals, especially mammals, accumulate information and remember things. They have, then, a rudimentary mind.

The problem of the mind and the brain is related to the controversy between idealism and materialism. Idealism has come to mean several variant philosophies mainly holding that true reality is some spiritual essence, some non-material form. Among such views is the absolute idealism of Hegel where something called Mind is gradually unfolding or evolving through a dialectical process, an inevitable progress over time. Hegel not only advocates a totally unacceptable belief in progress, but also in an essentially authoritarian view in which the State is a central figure in this evolution.

Then there is the subjective idealism of Bishop Berkeley which argues that ultimate reality comprises only that which is conceived or observed by a mind. Since not everything can be observed by human minds, this means that there must be a mind of god who sees everything, all a somewhat bizarre notion. For both these idealisms the ultimate reality is in some non-material entity - a mind, soul or god. There is no true reality independent of the mind. But as I have said there is a "real" world out there independent of any human, but each human sees the world through his idea of it and that idea is derived from the structure of the brain and the acquisition through the brain interaction with the environment of a world view. This may be an idealism of sorts in that it stresses that our perception of the world becomes a reality for us. This I suppose is a view with some affinity with Kant.

I believe one may reject materialism yet at the same time argue that the mind is not some mystical entity independent of brain, although it is to be distinguished from brain. Traditional materialism argues that reality is ultimately composed of isolated indivisible particles or "atoms" which have the quality of extension in space and duration in time. In anthropological theory this philosophy is expressed in views which find the reality of culture, that is, the fundamental moving or causal force in culture in two areas: 1) in the material objects of human manufacture - the physical tools employed and 2) the observed behavior of humans and particularly in those social institutions which are directly concerned with the production and distribution of material goods. This refers especially to the economy. Some materialists would emphasize extra cultural, but nevertheless, material phenomena such as population dynamics, genetics or the physical environment.

Critics of materialism suggest that it was more amenable to a nineteenth century notion of physics, but modern science has, especially in quantum theory, upset some scientific certainty in regard to physical laws, the nature of mechanics and matter. The latter may be seen as particles at one moment and waves at another. Some would say that the important characteristics of matter as extension in space and duration in time seem to evaporate into a sequence of forms and events.

Even if we grant the reality of some kind of atoms or particles in the traditional materialist manner, we must note that these particles have a distinct relationships to one another. They possess a structure or comprise a configuration of a relatively stable relationship to one another. Such stable patterns are non-material features which are clearly as much a part of the "ultimate reality" as the particles themselves. Reality is not merely a congeries of atomic particles. The non-material features of organization or configuration and, therefore, the laws of nature themselves are just as much a part of reality as the particles themselves. Indeed, as seems to be advocated by some observers of the natural world, it is possible that it is the relationships which are the important and fundamental entities. The materialist may point to the stone blocks as the ultimate units in a great cathedral, but the mentalist or idealist suggests that these blocks must be arranged in a specific design and that this is what creates the cathedral. Thus, organization and pattern are paramount.

One mentalist view in addition stresses that all any human knows about the world around him is processed through the brain, an instrument which organizes and categorizes the world. As has been pointed out above we see and act in relationship to a world of appearances. While we may remain skeptical of a subjective and objective idealist conception of the world we also must remain skeptical of the materialist view.

Many have deprecated the old arguments between idealists and materialists as unproductive and a peculiar obsession of Western minds. As particles may become waves and waves become particles so also "matter" and "idea" may be only aspects of the same ultimate reality. Or perhaps ultimate reality is just the "laws of nature."

In the past few pages I have tried to present a view of the age old body-mind problem. I don't pretend that what I have said is anything dramatic or original and indeed the whole essay may be easily dismissed as naive and confused. For myself I think I have in my senior years resolved the issue.

*****

Another source of new experience and new friendships while at Sockbridge was with the Society of Friends. A small meeting existed in nearby Northampton and there was a handful of Friends living in Amherst, especially there was Bill Scott who taught physics at Amherst College. Over the years which followed I had several associations with Friends and one thing has stood out and that is that Friends are not particularly friendly.

By age twelve I had come to accept a kind of New Testament Protestantism which was unitarian and strongly opposed to ritual, ornamentation and clergy. I have always entertained sympathy for Protestantism which I saw as a system of belief which furthered independent and free thought. I saw in the Reformation and subsequent developments the appearance of new ideas which stressed liberty and encouraged the development of a critical and scientific examination of our world. Protestantism was also free of hierarchy and centralized authority, of pomp, ritual and idolatry. I still think this has some truth, but I did not at the time realize that there was a darker and authoritarian side to Protestantism, . There was Luther and Calvin and Protestant participation in the persecution of dissenters. I did not appreciate the extent to which Protestantism in its search for legitimate grounding veers towards adherence to Biblical inerrancy and, thus, narrow minded and ignorant fundamentalism. All my experience had been with the so-called "liberal" Protestant denominations which seemed to share those positive characteristics that I saw. Unfortunately, it appears in this twenty first century that Protestantism has become increasingly a captive of this fundamentalism and those sects which advocate it are the ones who attract the most followers. I would attribute this to the increasing need to find a secure and certain foundation in an increasingly uncertain world, a security which is lacking in the "liberal" denominations. Further, the need for a security in fundamentalism arises in part out of the apparent decline in that which was once provided by the family, by friendships and neighborliness. Or put differently, adherence to this fundamentalist nonsense reflects a nostalgic desire either to return to or to maintain certain "old fashioned" or rural ways.

Psychologically I have been profoundly influenced by a Protestant ethic, which seems to have three important facets: work, guilt and personal responsibility. "Salvation" is attained through work, constructive, creative and "good" work. This , of course, is, as Max Weber emphasized, a feature which became a justifying ideology for capitalism. However, few capitalists have ever been much concerned with the "good" work so much as work to increase profit or they have defined good work as work for profit and personal aggrandizement. It is interesting to note the extent to which this so-called Protestant work ethic has been dismembered from its association with the religion. Today, in North America one finds innumerable Catholics tied to this ethic. In my own case, I have always been driven to be doing something "productive" and "not wasting time." In contrast, the Protestant white aristocracy of the old American South and the Protestant Boers of South Africa appear not to have been touched by this ethic. They laid all their menial tasks upon a slave population and devoted their time to riding their estates supervising and going on hunting expeditions. In my own case, guilt is probably the most potentially debilitating feature of a Protestant ethic. It readily causes excessive stress, inhibits action and "wastes time." It is, however, a clear indication that one has a moral sense or a social concern and a drive to do what is right. And it is the prod that seeks to keep one on the "right path." I have felt no little guilt concerning my negative attitude towards my parents and in many of my social relations.

Personal responsibility is most difficult to learn and adhere to, but if the world is to have decent social relations and care for the earth it should be a paramount requirement. Erich Fromm wrote in "Escape from Freedom" that the Protestant Reformation freed humankind from the authoritarianism of a domineering church and made each person responsible for his own salvation. That one is so left alone and given freedom is a frightening experience which provokes a flight from such freedom to new forms of authoritarianism - the everlasting arms of the loving father. Personal responsibility, guilt, and work are all closely interrelated. One's constructive work is a way of assuming personal responsibility. Failure in personal responsibility and in the freedom to act invokes guilt for wrong doing.

Roman Catholicism has always been anathema to me and in Massachusetts one had much exposure to it. Many of my early acquaintances were Catholics and some of them often harassed me for being a Protestant. At the same time some of the nicest people I have known in my later life have been Catholics. This creates a problem in which it is difficult to reconcile the individual practitioners with the system. For one thing, Catholicism does not seem to inculcate a hardnosed, skin flint attitude and so might make for a certain more easy going and hospitable person. Nevertheless, I cannot see how any rational person dedicated to the principles of freedom and justice can adhere to such an authoritarian, priest driven, and ritualistic religious system so filled with such utter nonsense and magic as the transforming of bread and wine into the body and blood of an alleged god or the notion that god could have a mother. Above all, is the belief that a man - the pope - can be in any way infallible, or that priests know best and can absolve one of "sins." So much of Romanist practice is pure mumbo jumbo and idol worship. In addition to this is the well known corruption of the system. How could an organization that professes the teachings of Christ be so wealthy and powerful, so responsible for so much torture and bloodshed throughout history or for such institutions as the Inquisition or the Index of forbidden books? Not only is it ritual hocus pocus, but it is also financial hocus pocus with a good portion of the hierarchy being engaged in weird sexual hanky panky to boot.

The Society of Friends provided a religion without clergy, without ritual or decor, free of the corruption brought by power and wealth. It taught the doctrine of the inner light, that all humans have a divine spark, and so should be treated accordingly. I enjoyed the freedom provided by the silent, unprogrammed meetings of Friends. As the years past, however, I began to question the whole Christian religion and religion in general.

*****

Among my fellow agricultural students at Stockbridge I acquired yet another group of friends, some of whom I remember with fondness and now wonder what ever became of them. I found the course work only mildly interesting, although I disliked agricultural engineering where we were expected to do varying kinds of work in blacksmithy, carpentry and auto mechanics. I should have realized by then that if one is to be a farmer he must also be a mechanic. That took me a couple of more years to appreciate and, once realized, led me out of any idea of farming as a career.

One of the requirements at Stockbridge was to work for six months on a farm. Thus, from April until October, 1942 I worked at the Storrow Farm in Lincoln. In part my motivation for working there was that I would be closest to Jean Smith. Storrow Farm was a 150 acre estate owned by the very wealthy Storrow family. They had a large apple orchard, a small market garden, some poultry and a herd of nine Guernsey cows. I used to get up at five every morning and go to the barn where I helped Mr Bush clean the stalls, feed and milk the cows by hand. After this, I went to breakfast and worked as an ordinary hand on the place until five in the afternoon.

I often went from Lincoln to Wayland to visit Jean. This was seven miles and I had to walk and try to hitch a ride to and from her house. I frequently did not get into bed on the nights I visited her until well after midnight and had to be on the job next morning at five. Sometimes I would almost fall asleep as I rested my head against a cow's flank and milked.

The noon hour was always a pleasant time because most of the hands gathered to talk, tell stories and joke. Especially memorable as a conversationalist was the elderly horse teamster, Dick Dumphy, who had a dry wit and enjoyed poking fun at those who took themselves too seriously.

In the fall I returned to Amherst and finished Stockbridge in the spring of 1943. At that time I went to work on a small dairy farm in Sherborn, Massachusetts. Here I finally realized that farming was not the occupation for me. This farm was owned by a Boston businessman. There were ten milking cows. I managed to foul up most everything here, although I believe I was not solely responsible for all the mistakes which occurred. I was asked to use an old milking machine which I found extremely diffi- cult to clean. This resulted in reports of high bacterial counts in the milk.

I was also to use a tractor which had no brakes and, while I was driving it down an inclined pathway, I lost control of it and it ran out into the middle of the highway and turned over in a poison ivy thicket. Luckily no one was coming down the road at the time or I might not have survived the accident. After this I was sent to make a fence line, but didn't have large enough posts. Further, there was no proper device for putting up barbed wire. I could only tighten the wire with a hammer. Finally, I became literally sick of the whole business and left.

For a few months thereafter I worked as a pasteurizer in a dairy plant in Waltham. During this time I was called up for the draft and had to visit the Draft Board to explain my conscientious objection. At that time I based my objection on the New Testament especially the Sermon on the Mount as well as principles of the Society of Friends although I hardly remember anything which transpired during the visit. My father, a war veteran and conservative, most graciously spoke to the draft board in my favour.

I was granted a 4E classification as a conscientious objector which meant that I had to report to a "civilian public service camp." On my twentieth birthday I appeared at the Big Flats, New York camp run by the American Friends Service Committee for the Selective Service System. According to the general arrangement the so-called three historic peace churches - Friends, Mennonites, and Brethren - took on responsibility for operating these camps within rules which were laid down by the Selective Service System. Thus these churches were expected to be policemen for the military establishment.

At Big Flats we worked in a tree nursery and also engaged in thinning out trees in publicly owned lands nearby. But Big Flats was primarily a staging area for ultimately sending CO conscripts to various other camps. I was assigned to Elkton, Oregon where

I first worked on a crew making a forestry road. This was followed by six months on a land survey in an antelope refuge in southeastern Oregon. Actually there were parts of this experience I enjoyed. I especially liked the desert conditions and being in the midst of ranch country. Later, I was in a camp for tree planting and fighting forest fires. I managed to spend some time as a cook which was at least somewhat enjoyable. Of course, we were supposed to be doing work of national importance and many CO's eagerly sought out the most nasty and dangerous jobs they could obtain within the system in order to prove that they weren't slackers and cowards. They went to become orderlies in mental hospitals or smoke jumpers fighting forest fires or experimental guinea pigs in laboratories. The rest of us stayed in the camps, unimpressed by the entire arrangement. We were the "whiners" and complainers opposed to the concentration camp existence. No matter what one's task, a conscientious objector received no compensation, although the "historic peace churches" did give us $2.50 a month, our board, room and laundry. The camps, incidentally, were old CCC camp sites - long dormitories heated by wood stoves at either end.

In CPS (Civilian Public Service) I was exposed

to many new ideas and interesting people. One fellow led me to Nietzsche who impressed me for many of his wild statements which so often had the clear ring of truth. I sometimes felt sympathy for his idea of an aristocracy of intelligent and free men beyond the common crowd and common notions of good and evil. I thought of his denunciation of orthodox values and their degenerate nature, of the stress on the strong minded person who could rise above the mass. There could be men who were truly free. Such thoughts at these times were soothing to my long standing resentments; they had a cathartic effect.

While I was still too young to vote in 1944, I supported Norman Thomas, the Socialist candidate for president (on his fifth try). However, I was becoming more interested in the potential impact of the state in a socialist system and its threat to individual freedom. I had initially been influenced by Marx and in certain respects I still am. Indeed, I spent a good part of the summer of 1943 slogging through his "Capital" ,vol I. His critique of capitalism was most convincing and I would still agree that capitalism provokes alienation and exploitation. But in 1944 in the little library of the Elkton CPS camp I discovered a publication called "Why?" which advocated anarchism - a free, socialist society.

I soon came to realize that socialists, including the Marxists, did not appreciate the fact that power has more than economic sources and motivation. And on reading Bakunin I accepted his critique of Marxism. The dictatorship of the proletariat could only be a dictatorship of bureaucrats and party hacks. To dominate others, to manipulate and exploit people could be accomplished not only by economic factors as Marx advocated, but knowledge and managerial skills could be employed to these ends as well. In many cultures religious specialists controlled affairs by their alleged greater knowledge. Men who were not wealthy often gain control of the military and take over control of people if only because of their drive and love of power. The problem in human societies was not exclusively one of economic differences and the distribution of wealth. The problem in human societies was also one of power. That is, power as domination over others. There is also power of a positive nature which is a kind of power in equality in which one exerts his influence by rational argument, or works with others in mutual action. The assertion of one's freedom is another form of positive power.

One struggles against restraint and uses power to say "no." Anarchism opposes power as domination and manipulation and favors power in equality and as an assertion of freedom. While it is often accused of having an extremely optimistic and rosy view of human nature, in fact, one can say that anarchists do not trust that nature. They see the immanent dangers of the drive for power and necessity of curtailing it.

Anarchism is a social and political theory developed in 19th century Europe. In it human freedom and rights of the individual are paramount. Thus, in anarchist theory, the first premise is something which Josiah Warren called the sovereignty of the individual and from this it follows that government and the state, as the most oppressive of institutions, should be abolished. At the same time other institutions are equally oppressive such as the church, the patriarchal family, and any system which appears to enshrine 'irrational' authority. Anarchism is egalitarian and anti-hierarchical. Discrimination based on alleged race or on sex is always anathema. Above all domination is the chief enemy.

The immediate reaction to any notion that the state and government are expendable is usually one of total amazement and disbelief. Governments are, it is said, absolutely essential for the preservation of order, for keeping the peace and protecting property and the individual. The anarchists reply that the state and its apparatus of maintenance, the government, are everywhere in the hands of a small ruling group, a privileged elite separated by its formation, status and organization from the population as a whole. This group collectively monopolizes political decisions. In some polities it may constitute an entrenched and self-perpetuating class. Indeed, this was the character of almost all states until a couple of centuries ago. In other more open systems such as democracy, there is a greater circulation or regular turnover of member-ship in this ruling group, so that dynasties or other kinds of closed classes of rulers do not ordinarily occur. This, of course, contributes to the illusion of equality of power in a democracy and obscures the division between rulers and ruled.

Democracy adds to the illusion of freedom and equality by proclaiming the idea of majority rule. However, such rule is a rare occurrence in any democracy. A large percentage of the population do not participate in voting because of indifference or frustration. And where there are several candidates the victor receives only the largest of all the votes, which is most of the time only a minority. Then we have the more fundamental problem of the rule of the majority. Why should 50.1% be able to impose their will on an opposing 49.9% or, for that matter, even on an opposing one per cent? What is sacred about a majority and what is ethical about forcing a minority to accept majority opinion?

Fundamental to both government and the state is the employment of violence to enforce the law. This may variously be viewed as either the imposition of the will of the ruling group or a device to maintain order. In fact states and governments fulfill all these functions by enforcing the law. Theorists on the so-called left, and especially anarchists, have emphasized that the paramount and ultimate end of all law enforcement is to benefit the ruling interests, particularly those of property even though there may be positive side effects such as keeping the peace. They would further emphasize that the existence of the state is conducive of strife and conflict. As a system based upon the use of violence it thereby legitimizes and incites it. The state is further predicated upon the assumption that some should be bosses giving orders while others should be subordinates. Authority is in no sense based upon any rational considerations such as intelligence, knowledge or competence. Such a situation can only irk the subordinates and frustrate them and, thus, become yet another provocation of violence. Democratic systems may ameliorate the condition, but they do not cure it.

By their nature state and government discourage, if they do not outlaw, the natural voluntary cooperation amongst people and seek to make the populace dependent upon them. Personal responsibility and effort are discouraged. People are encouraged to say "Let the government do it" or "Why doesn't the government do it?"

Anarchists clearly oppose Thomas Hobbes' view that society without government is nasty and brutish. They set him on his head and argue that the world would be more peaceful and amenable to cooperation if the state were removed. And, clearly the anthropological record does not support Hobbes. Stateless societies seem less violent and brutish than those with the state. It has been state controlled societies that were responsible for the deaths of over one hundred million people in the wars of the 20th century.

Above all the state and government are organizations for war. No more efficient organization for war has been developed. The state is a predator engaging in a Darwinian like struggle against opposing states for more power, more territory. Of course, in the battle most states eventually must resign themselves to impotency and to become mere satellites of the most powerful. Presently there is the unusual situation in which only one superstate exists, the great American empire. Others are primarily its lackeys; a few attempt the impossible task of neutrality and a handful have the audacity to oppose.

In place of the old system anarchism advocates self regulation and voluntary cooperation. Social relations are to be carried out through free contractual agreements of mutual or equal benefit to all parties involved. For Proudhon mutualism was a basic cornerstone of anarchy and both he and Bakunin favoured a kind of federalism designed to facilitate relations between increasingly larger and more widespread and all inclusive groups. The initial building blocks of the federalist plan are local face to face groups either neighbors or persons of the same occupation. Such groups form and concern themselves with achieving their specified goals. For example, in a local area there might be organized a cooperative society for the care of roads, one for fire fighting, one for health and so on. In order to facilitate these ends they federate with others to form regional federations and these in turn may form yet greater federations. In each case the power invested in the organized group decreases as one ascends the levels of integration. As Bakunin said the system was to be "built from the bottom up and not from the top down." Each member of a federation has a right to withdraw if in disagreement with the majority.

All this may be seen as quite utopian and impossible to work. It is true that such an arrangement must depend upon the assumption of much personal responsibility and a sense of cooperation amongst people which can only be generated by education. One cannot expect to rely on the existing emphasis upon competition, conflict and the drive for power that are corner stones of contemporary society and evolve a cooperative community.

While I have subscribed to the anarchist critique of society for almost sixty years I recognize that the weakest part of the argument is the kind of society - that voluntary, mutualist society - one could have as an alternative. Such a system would be especially difficult to arrange in urban, congested areas. Anarchism has worked in cases of small face to face groups.

Even so one wonders if it would soon degenerate into the same old thing. But above all is the practical impossibility of creating such a society. No state has ever abdicated itself, nor would it. Modern states are fantastic juggernauts. As I said at a much later time, we may be anarcho-cynicalists fighting for the right even knowing that it is impossible.

In the latter part of my CPS days I started a small mimeographed periodical, " The Rebel Clarion," which became a voice of opposition within the camp to the whole CPS arrangement. Three colleagues and I produced about five issues before we were all moved out of the camp due to the ending of the war.

The end of hostilities did not bring release from the camps. Several individuals merely walked out, but there were a few of us who remained and refused to work. I was among these and was sent as a result to a government run camp in Lapine, Oregon. The Friends Service Committee was attempting not to get their hands too dirty and to avoid as much disciplinary action as it could. So it passed individuals like myself off to government run facilities which could seek to punish me properly. I no sooner landed in Lapine than two FBI agents visited and arrested me for refusing to work and so violating the Selective Service Act.

I was taken to Portland and placed in the county jail. Fortunately there was the Reverend Snyder, a Methodist minister, who lived in Portland and was a great supporter of war resistance. He provided the $300 bail so that I could be released and await trial. He pulled the bills out of his pocket in a most perfunctory manner and dropped them on the desk in front of the official. I spent one night in the jail which I can say was not a particularly pleasant place. The food was atrocious. 'Dinner' was a plate of soggy, unsalted boiled macaroni and breakfast a bowl of oatmeal with no milk. The guards bragged that people in their jail gained lots of weight. With such a starchy diet and no exercise what else could one expect if you ate all that stuff.

While awaiting the trial I worked as a busboy in a local restaurant. After three or four months my trial came up and the charges were dismissed. The judge who had been known as quite hardnosed about law breaking conscientious objectors (in the past he had sent several to jail for five year terms) now made an about face. He decided that I had been illegally transferred from Big Flats to Elkton and Lapine, that the Selective Service Act made no provision for such movements. Therefore, I was free to go home. It seems quite likely that now that the war was over the judge and others were just plain tired of wasting time on these objectors. However, I certainly did not object.

I mentioned above that I met many interesting people in CPS, but perhaps I should say that I met an immense variety of people, some of whom influenced me considerably. Others, and there were many, were Bible pounding fundamentalists with whom I initially argued until blue in the face. Finally, I learned that one cannot debate with such people and gave up trying. I had long and fruitful discussions with John McCandless who had been a newspaper reporter and city editor in Pennsylvania and with Barton Clausen. One of the people who influenced me most in CPS was David Fawcett who had come from Fletcher Park, Wyoming. This was a small community in the Laramie Mountains west of Wheatland. Before CPS and, then again when it ended, Fawcett lived with his wife in a one room log cabin and worked on various jobs such as logging, ranching and school teaching. He did some writing although none of it was ever published. Further, he attempted to derive an income from making violins. Fawcett himself had been raised in the Society of Friends and his chief influence was Henry David Thoreau. I decided to try to follow his example but since I had no money I would first have to work at any jobs I could find.

I went from Portland to Laramie where I began to work in a lumberyard. From this I soon escaped to go into a bakery. Here I was put on the bread making shift. One of my assignments was to go through the bread dough and pick out the rat droppings. I was also supposed to remove the baked bread from the moving trays in the oven, but I never could get used to this since it` was easy to get burned. They then put me on the night shift making cakes and pastries. But I found staying up all night difficult and moved on to work for a few weeks in a Safeway where I got into an argument with the manager and quit. I hung around Laramie for a couple of months reading Turgenev novels and other material from the local Carnegie library.

Finally, I fled again to my grandfather's farm back in Weston. Fawcett had suggested that teaching in a rural school might put me in a right direction. Thus while at the farm I applied for Summer School at the University of Wyoming where with the courses during the summer I could qualify as an elementary school teacher. In Wyoming, schools were scattered widely and there were a great number located on ranches for the children of a given ranch.

After the Summer School I attempted to find a likely position with some difficulty. Finally, I was approached by a rancher who lived about thirty miles outside Wheatland and north of Laramie. He had two children ages eight and ten. I accepted the position and went to visit the county school superintendent who gave me about thirty books and a pile of papers. I was supposed to start teaching the next day. Not only was I a complete greenhorn, but I had also prepared nothing and knew nothing at all of what was in the text books for the pupils.

I met the family in Wheatland and we proceeded to go out to the ranch. Before we arrived it had already begun to be dark so that my first impressions of the place were a bit unusual. Rounded smooth black hills hovered about; they were called "hogbacks." The road wound around in a canyon between the hogbacks out on an open meadow. In the moonlight a clump of cottonwoods was revealed. Here was an old school house made of squared off logs and divided into three rooms. This was to be my home. One room was reserved for storing salt and linseed cake for livestock. There was plenty of room in the remaining two for me and both a shepherd's stove for cooking and a large potbellied stove for warmth.

The next morning I had an opportunity to get my bearings. The ranch house and school were about a quarter mile down the dirt road. I managed to muddle through the first day and for two or three weeks thereafter I spent about twelve hours a day on school work. After teaching barely a week who should turn up for a visit but the county school superintendent. While I fumbled around making an effort to act school teacher she sat in the back of the room staring at me for two solid hours. I found, however, that the kids were as disturbed about the visit as I was. When she got up to leave she smiled and told me I was doing all right. I don't think she expected much.

I began to enjoy the position, the pupils and the surroundings. Often we would go off on horseback to various interesting sites, once to fish for rainbow trout in a stocked pond. On route we would sometimes encounter a coyote or two; mule deer on hearing our approach would, after their usual fashion, pop up and down over the brush and rocks to safety. There were squawking magpies and hawks that silently soared over head rising and falling in the wind currents. Once and a while a rattle snake warned us to stay away. One time while riding across a flat space we encountered some high dried grass which contained little seeds in pods and they rattled like a rattle snake. My horse didn't enjoy that sound at all and suddenly took off across the field.

The fall deer hunting season proved an interesting experience. Until then the road to the ranch had always been quiet, but with the beginning of the season there seemed to be a continuous rumble of pick ups as they moved along in search of their prey. A barrage of high-powered rifles echoed between the hills. The "soldiers" stalked along the stony slopes hiding behind a boulder here or a buckbush there. They were royally garbed, clothed in brilliant red hats, fancy shirts daubed with scarlet and thick leather belts which supported glistening knives. All day long the trucks and cars maneuvered up and down the road before my cabin. The red daubed riflemen were like a military parade. They camped where they pleased and took what they pleased. It was an invasion and one questioned the advisability of going out on the road.

After a while I detected the return of the first attackers. For some the red now covered their hands or blotched their pants - signs of their success. The backs of trucks carried the corpses of the defeated and this was to go on for two weeks. It was not any search of needed food. It was recreation and war play which even had a few rules and umpires - the game wardens. Soon, however, I learned that not everyone abided by the rules. Out on the side of one barren hill I found a buck - dead after having been wounded. The hunter had not wanted to bother stalking it, so left it to go off out of sight and die. I dressed and skinned the animal for my own use and took it back to my cabin placing it in the storeroom only to have it stolen a couple of days later.

School regulations seemed a hodge podge of contradictions. A state law prohibits teaching religion in the school. Yet the school had its Bible and I was encouraged to read from it. Teachers were not to express personal opinions regarding world affairs, but that didn't stop the state from taking the opportunity to fill the minds of the pupils with all sorts of patriotic ballyhoo.

There was a course in so-called world history which annoyed me. It commenced with "early" man, moved on to Greece and Rome with a little of Babylon and Egypt thrown in. We then turned to a general review of Europe for the ensuing several hundred years, while the rest of the world was ignored. By 1700 we were in America - the United States of America, that is - and all the rest of the world disappeared entirely from then on. While in Laramie I had read Spengler's "Decline of the West" and, influenced by it, had developed a few definite ideas about history. For instance, I thought history taught in discrete units such a English history or American history made no sense. The history of humankind was a whole and one should seek to blend it together. Further, one should not emphasize the modern over the ancient; both were equally important. Civilizations were born, matured and they all eventually died. The latter observation was one of the issues which eventually lead to major problems in teaching here, because I told the children that America may be on top of the world now, but like Greece and Rome it too would decline and disappear.

When I first went to Wyoming the west impressed me deeply - the great open spaces, the hard beauty of the land. There was freedom; the air was fresh. Cowboy culture intrigued me. All of this is still so. Nothing equals a horseback ride into the open plains. However, I have learned a bit in the last half century that creates an ambivalence within me about the West. I have learned how the aboriginal population was exposed to a holocaust at the expense of the Euro-American settler-intruders. I have learned how those who survived were herded onto reservations and deprived of their self respect and livelihood. I have learned that an important means of subduing these indigenous peoples was to destroy their chief source of sustenance, the buffalo. And by doing so another goal was achieved: the Western grasslands were made free for cattle herds and safe therefore for the beef industry.

Finally, I have learned that while ranching may encourage individual responsibility and an emphasis on personal freedom, at the same time it is clearly associated with a rather unpleasant macho or he-man view of the world which tends to have a callous view of life and living things. And that emphasis on freedom is countered by a glorification of the "American way" and intolerance of "foreigners."

The ranch family I stayed with were a most friendly and gracious people, but they were also very conservative and narrow minded. Once when we were in town to shop a couple of black men walked down the sidewalk and the rancher's wife exclaimed, "What are these people doing in our town?" I noticed a couple of books from the local library written by Norman Thomas which were on the kitchen table. They had taken them out to check up on any connection I might have with radical ideas. They knew I was acquainted with David Fawcett and were aware of his background: "You know where he was during the war?" - referring to the conscientious objector camp. I did not tell them that I, too, was there. I, also, had not saluted the flag with the children during morning school exercises and this was particularly damning. Everything soon erupted into an unpleasant climax where I was accused of being unpatriotic, of trampling on the American flag and teaching that other countries were superior to the United States. I cannot recall whether they asked me to leave or whether I volunteered to do so. In any case I did leave in late January, 1948. Following is from a letter I wrote to the local representative of the school board:

Dear Mr Mylet:
    It is with regret that I must inform you that I have been forced to leave my

position at the Rosentreter school. Early last month trouble arose regarding the flag. I had told Larry and Myrtle at the commencement of the year that they might salute the flag when so inclined. Although I respect the flag and the country, it has not been part of my belief to exercise open or outward expression in religious worship or such respect as making allegiance to the flag. I had thought this breach was mended when I asked the children each morning for the flag salute.

However, through different sources in the past couple of weeks I have learned that I have been teaching Larry and Myrtle that other countries were superior to this one, that the United States was no good; that I have taught my own personal beliefs in school; that I have spit, stamped upon and otherwise defamed the flag; that I and my friends must all be 'nihilists' and 'socialists'; that I possess 'screwy' ideas and other inferences almost implying that I am a carnate devil, needing to be shipped off of the earth.

What I have said about other countries, other peoples in relation to the United States has been this - that in many ways the Greek civilization was superior to the current one. I have said that the Scandinavian countries have the highest percentage of literacy. I have pointed out that there are countries just as democratic as the United States; I have stated that the greatest musicians and some of the greatest scientists and medical men were Germans. What I have attempted and, apparently failed to point out, is that all the people in the world regardless of race or color all do the same good things, the same bad things - all are essentially the same. In short the only thing I have tried to say is - there is no master race. I have tried to present arguments against ideas championed by men such as Hitler.

Regarding the teaching of religion or personal beliefs in school I can only say that such an assumption has been drawn from a complete misconstruing of the above ideas. Also, I have in the sixth grade had to teach about the Moslem civilization and the Protestant Reformation, wherein to my knowledge I made no partisan statements.

To be sure, there have been occasions where Larry asked my opinion about a subject and I told him. One such question referred to military schools and I stated I didn't believe in them.

It has been rumoured that I have spit and trampled upon the American flag. That is false. Not only have I never done such a thing, but the thought has never entered my head.

To my knowledge none of my friends are nihilists or socialists and I profess none of these doctrines. Neither am I a Communist or a Nazi. I have no use for these concepts. I admit that my ideas are different, but I do not thereby see that they are insane. I believe in respecting and trying to understand everyone's ideas. Like anyone else I believe in peace and freedom. I have not, however, ever found any theories wherein these ideals might be inaugurated. I have had to console myself with believing that each man must act as nearly in accord with the Golden Rule as he can. This entails broadening the human understanding of one man by another. It involves respect for all men. That is what I believe.

Had I realized such thoughts would involve me in numerous unpleasant relationships while teaching I would never have thought of the occupation. I suppose I should have explained my ideas to the Rosentreters in September, but I did not dream such thoughts would so entangle me.

Before this situation arose I enjoyed every minute of my stay with the Rosentreters. I know 1 learned a great deal and enjoyed myself immensely with Larry and Myrtle. The Rosentreters own homey hospitality could not be surpassed.

Sincerely

This episode was one of the most disturbing in my life and one of my major regrets, not only because the Rosentreters were such good people, but because I was not completely open and honest about the affair. In my letter I said nothing that wasn't true, but I left unsaid relevant points that should have been said. I never mentioned that I was a war objector or that while I wasn't a nihilist or socialist I did hold many radical and anarchistic opinions. My letter was entirely too sweet; I portrayed myself as being in favour of motherhood and apple pie.

I know that the Rosentreters continued to despise me for decades thereafter, because once, passing through Wheatland, I knocked on their door, but no one was home, so I left a copy of my recently published book, "The Role of the Horse in Man's Culture." They never responded.

Following this fiasco I returned again to my refuge, my grandfather's farm in Weston, Mass. Here I worked for a year and a half. At the end of the work day I tried my hand at writing a kind of autobiographical novel which when read today seems utterly bitter and angry. I had been reading Joyce's "Ulysses" and tried writing in a stream of consciousness manner. During this time as well I read several 'classic' novels. I enjoyed D. H. Lawrence's descriptions of life in English coal mining communities. For a short time I was intrigued by his view of the sexual act as a kind of mystical experience. "Moby Dick" seemed to me a really great novel, although I was disappointed in Melville's other writing. I read Dostoevsky and Tolstoy. "Hunger" and "Children of the Age" by Knut Hamsun impressed me. As I recall the latter involved the struggle between a rather poor aristocrat and an up and coming prosperous capitalist. My sympathies were with the poor aristocrat and I saw the book as condemnation of capitalism and support for an agrarian tradition in a Nietzschean like vein. Two Czech authors were of interest. Jaroslav Hasek wrote "The Good Soldier Svejk," a most entertaining satire of all military organization and war which provided numerous ways one might undermine any war effort and not be suspected. One never knew whether Svejk was deliberately messing up everything or if he did so out of stupidity. The other writer, Franz Kafka, was of a totally different cast. I especially enjoyed his portrayal of victims in "The Castle" and "The Trial" for it seemed to me that they portrayed what life was really like: One was hopelessly ensnared in a bureaucratic nightmare and could never know why one was being "tried." Unforgettable is Kafka's short story, "The Metamorphosis," in which a man sees himself transformed into an insect. Oddly enough I later learned that both Hasek and Kafka were anarchists.

In the past I had read only a little of Henry David Thoreau which now seems rather odd since he was the main inspiration, for what at that time was my desire to move off into a wilderness and live in a cabin writing great works. At any rate I now steeped myself in all of Thoreau's writings. I recall that when I was at the ranch school I had mentioned Thoreau to the Rosentreters and they reacted quite negatively to his ideas as I described them. I would certainly place Thoreau among the half dozen writers who have most impressed me. Another in this category was Proudhon and I especially liked his "General Idea of the Revolution of the Nineteenth Century." Other anarchists that I read less extensively included Kropotkin, especially his "Mutual Aid: a factor of Evolution" and also Bakunin who seems to have written a multitude of essays which were never finished. But a major new discovery was Ruth Benedict's "Patterns of Culture" which converted me to anthropology. Among other things I now saw how anthropology was a reply to my parents and to all the 'red necks,' demonstrating the error of racism, confounding their ethnocentrism, revealing that war and capitalism were not necessary and universal features of every human society. All these narrow-minded people would be shown the error of their ways through anthropology.

I applied for admission to Boston University which at that time did not have a separate anthropology program; it was a minor companion to sociology. I was not to begin my freshman year until September, 1949. I would be sort of an anomaly because I would be twenty five years old - an old student - but not a returning veteran. Like most students a major problem at university would be finances. Happily I was able to have free board and room with my parents, so that my meager savings could be directed entirely to tuition and bus fares. From my sophomore year onward I was able to obtain scholarships and those along with part time work in a grocery store and, later, as a janitor in a bank allowed me to squeak through to graduation.

Before entering Boston University, however, I made some rare sexual conquests. I had had no "date" with any girl for about a year. Now I met a young divorcee, four years older than me, who was a secretary at the CARE office in Boston where I knew the director who was a brother of a CPS colleague. I eventually built up sufficient courage to ask her for a date, which in no time led to my loss of virginity. I know I am not the first person to have been "seduced" by an older and more knowledgeable woman, although I do not know whether this was truly seduction. We carried on for a few months, but she had other problems including two young children. It was she who had the wisdom to end the affair. After that I had a few other relationships.

Barton Clausen, who had been a friend of mine in the CPS camp, had also dreams of following David Fawcett's ideas, but instead of going to the West and Wyoming, he purchased a farm in southern Vermont. I visited him there on several occasions. There were other former conscientious objectors in the general vicinity as well as a more well known person, Scott Nearing. Barton never made a success of it. He never had more than one cow and a vegetable garden and tried to earn enough to keep alive by driving a school bus. It seems to me that the life he espoused was in a so many ways radically different from the suburban, middle class life he had known. I suspect also that the funds for the farm purchase had been acquired from his rather well to do father. Within a few years he was a not unsuccessful businessman which was probably a more appropriate career. Eventually I lost track of him, but learned a few years ago that both he and his wife had died. This was also the fate of David Fawcett who may have committed suicide. Lost, too, was John McCandless from emphysema. Half of those I considered good friends in the conscientious objector camp have now died, but I suppose one could expect no better given that experience was almost sixty years ago. I think we all had visions of making some positive dent in the world. Rick Chiarito thought of becoming a symphony orchestra conductor. In fact he became a University of Nevada librarian. John McCandless would be a poet while Dave Fawcett, Bart Clausen, Omar Bose and I would find the wilderness cabin and at least some of us intended to write profound works. But none of this would ever come to fruition. We would never make that dent and I suppose the same is true of more than 99% of other people as well.

CHAPTER III
Finding Myself

At Boston University I commenced a new life which now appeared to have a more realistic direction. No longer did I think of writing the Great Work in some wilderness cabin. I had only begun the year when I was involved in another love affair, this time with a fellow student in a history of western civilization course. Jane Lepore was the daughter of a Newton fireman who was the son of Italian immigrants. Her mother was from a lower middle class old New England and English family. We seemed to find many things in common. We began attending square dances and this soon expanded to international folk dancing. There was Ted Sannella's Friday nights in Cambridge and Joe Perkins in mid week in Belmont. Later when I started graduate school at Cornell we went to Roger Knox's combination square and folk dance where we danced with Gene and Vera Donefer. Gene later became director of McGill International at McGill University. We carried on with the dancing for several years. Even when we went to the Sudan we attended Scottish country dancing at the Sudan Club under the direction of the manager of the local Barclay's bank. I particularly liked some of the Scottish dances, but there were too many picky people who were so concerned about form that they destroyed all the fun. I have noticed with other activities involving the British that the main focus is not enjoyment, but rather with following a lot of strict rules and regulations. This is what happens with British pony and horse type organizations.

I enjoyed most of the course work at Boston University. I was introduced to anthropology by Linvill Watson who was not the most dynamic of speakers, but since he was one of two anthropologists at the university I took other courses with him as well. We became acquainted with each other and Jane and I used to go with him to parties put on by the African students. I also had a course on Southwestern Indians from Leland Wyman. Al Zalinger, a student of Robert Merton, exposed me to a considerable dosage of functionalist theory. I later learned that Al was originally in the Worker's Socialist Party, but apparently now had given up Marxism for functionalism. For some reason he never completed his PhD at Columbia. A year course in biology was taught by BU's most famous biologist, a man with an international reputation as a great researcher, but he certainly wasn't a teacher. Psychology with Prof. Pinard was, I thought, rather an odd course and I suspected a racist note. Another Psychology course with Prof. Thibeault consisted of his reading from the text book which was hardly enlightening.

The most rewarding of all the courses at Boston University was a year of the Great Books with Angelo Bertocci. We covered "The Iliad," The Old Testament, Dante's "Divine Comedy," a Shakespeare play, Dostoevsky's "Brothers Karamazov," Joyce's "Ulysses" among others that I have since forgotten. Bertocci was a dynamic teacher, the best at Boston University. He was able in his lectures to enthrall you with each of these works - certainly not at all an easy task. Always when the bell rang for the end of class he would still continue on and everyone seemed to hang on to his every word while students for the next class lined up outside waiting.

Psychology was a secondary interest of mine during the years at B.U. I belonged to the Psychology club and we visited mental hospitals and played around with Rhine's cards attempting to find some validation for the idea of extra sensory perception.

Although there were twenty or more of us who regularly worked with the cards no one ever came up with anything that would indicate some extra sensory perception.

Since I wasn't a veteran I was forced to take physical education. Here I found that I could play away the time with badminton which was at least a passable activity. I was able to complete the BA degree in three years. As part of my degree work I wrote an honours thesis on "The Functions of the Kwakiutl Potlach" and graduated in the Spring of 1952 complete with a Phi Beta Kappa key and the BA cum laude.

Jane and I went together for almost four years before marrying. One problem which had to be sorted out was the religious issue. Her mother had on her marriage converted to Roman Catholicism, the religion of her husband, so that Jane and her sister were reared in this church. A year or so after we had first met I managed to convince her to leave that religion, to which she was not strongly attached anyway. When I graduated from BU Jane still had another year to finish and I had not applied in time to any graduate school to commence in 1952. I, therefore, spent the next year working in a factory which made cloth. I worked in the inspection department where I had to bring bolts of cloth to the inspectors to examine for flaws. When winter came there was little work in the factory so I, as a more recent employee, was layed off. Following this I participated in a cigarette survey where I went around asking people what kind of cigarette they smoked. In the latter I often got an inside picture of how the poor in Boston lived since I was assigned routes in West Roxbury and the North End. At the same time I was investigating universities for graduate study. One of my major concerns was to obtain financial assistance. At the time, too, I had an interest in American Indians. Cornell University offered me the best arrangement so I accepted to go there.

In the summer of 1953 Jane and I were married by Ken Patton, a well known Universalist minister, at the Universalist Meeting House in Boston. I had come to know Ken when he used to have discussion groups at the meeting house. He was a humanist, pacifist and a radical. Therefore our wedding ceremony was completely within the humanist mode, without religious falderal. I had no belief in the confirmation by the state and by religion of my partnership with Jane and at the time felt that I could tolerate the arrangement made by Patton. Merely to start living together in the early 50's would have entailed strong opposition from both our parents and I do not believe Jane would have been very comfortable with it.

Jane obtained a job in the Cornell library which was an essential for us if we were to survive since my savings were meager and Cornell's scholarship hardly did more than pay for the tuition. We moved into a small two room furnished apartment in which we had to share the bath with two other tenants. Here we lived for three years. Our biggest feasts were pot roast or chicken wings. Jane was always a first rate cook and could always be counted on to turn out the best with the least. It is to be regretted that her culinary art has never been enjoyed by a wider population. That is, for the most part she has only been able to share her considerable gourmet ability with me. I am often impressed by how frequently the really great things in life are, for one reason or another, only shared by a tiny minority. In our first year at Cornell we were not well received and just about completely ignored. Everyone else was associated with some area program, but I was not. Finally, in our second year new people arrived and life was more sociable.

It was possible at Cornell to work directly for a PhD and avoid the masters. However, I thought that perhaps I should get the masters degree just in case I did not finish the PhD. Thus, I had to develop a masters thesis. I was impressed with Morris Opler's idea of themes in culture and was also now interested in the Dene of northern Canada. Therefore, I prepared the thesis on themes in Slave (the name of one group of Dene) culture under the direction of Robert J. Smith, who actually was a Japan specialist, but as a new faculty member I imagine he was given anomalies like me. Bob Smith was always extremely easy to work with and he was also available which is more than one can say about so many university bigwigs. I acquired an MA in 1954 and proceeded to the PhD.

My interests had changed considerably, as I began to feel that there was not much one could do with American Indians. I found that the Middle East was little researched providing many opportunities for exploring new problems. The Berbers of Morocco, a highly decentralized society, attracted my attention. The problem here was that at this time Morocco was undergoing considerable strife over the French rule and it was not the best place to attempt fieldwork. I read extensively on Middle Eastern culture and Islamic societies and eventually decided to turn further eastward to Egypt. Of course, another problem was that no one at Cornell was a specialist in this area, but I proceeded ahead anyway. To attempt to make up for this shortcoming I investigated other universities, but was unable to make any satisfactory arrangements.

In the summer of 1955 with a grant from Cornell we went to Washington, D. C. where I took a course in Jeruselem Arabic at Georgetown University. The instructor, Majed F. Said, was without a doubt the best teacher that I have ever had in my career. Unfortunately I understand that he acquired some terminal illness and died at rather an early age. In this course we had to spend a great deal of time listening to tapes and repeating the sounds of words. I assume I became extremely loud in pronouncing the Arabic, because I was often asked by the supervisor to be a bit quieter since I was disturbing the others.

To acquire funds for research required writing proposals to places such the Ford Foundation. Much academic research requires one to learn how to become an astute beggar. I sent Ford a proposal, but was rejected primarily because I was not at an institution where Middle Eastern studies was available. In after thought it was probably just as well that I did not have the Ford grant since on eventually arriving in Egypt we spent several months dealing in one fashion or another with the Suez crisis and ultimately being told by Egyptian authorities that village research would not be permitted.

I do not now recall how I learned of the American University at Cairo, but in any case I wrote to them inquiring if they had any teaching positions in anthropology and it was my great luck that they responded positively and I was able to accept an appointment there for a three year term.

However, before describing those wonderful years in Cairo, I must recount my activities at Cornell. In my first year at Cornell I took a couple of seminars as well as course work. One seminar with Bryce Ryan dealt with theory. I researched an extensive paper on the cultural pattern idea in anthropology. This view held that each culture tends to constitute an integrated configuration or orientation which gives it a distinctive character. I presented a critique beginning as far back as Montesquieu in his "Spirit of the Laws" and proceeding to contemporary anthropologists Kroeber, Benedict and Morris Opler. This seminar also introduced me to Talcott Parsons who was THE great sociological theorist of that time. I, however, found it difficult to see that he was saying anything much different from A. R. Radcliffe-Brown. One of the benefits of Parsons was to provide one with the opportunity to become acquainted with such classic authors as Emile Durkheim, Max Weber, and Vilfredo Pareto. Another seminar with Alan Holmberg was on cultural change and I presented material on the fur trade and its impact upon the Slave Indians. Holmberg was a very kindly person, but his lecture room delivery was most painful. As a contribution to the seminar he read through notes taken from Homer Barnett's recently published book, "Innovation."

In my second year I was a teaching assistant in an introductory anthropology course and had to take about thirty students for a weekly meeting, as well as correct their papers and examinations. One aspect of teaching I could never get used to was making up examinations and accurately correcting them. Long essays were particularly overwhelming, evaluations being entirely too subjective. Ideally, one would hope that all grading and examinations could be dispensed with and we should be left with the personal respon-

sibility of the student to acquaint himself with the
material with the assistance of the instructor.

I later participated in several interesting seminars.
In one I reviewed the development of the concept
of culture area while in another I made an analysis
of "social integration," particularly as it applied to
anthropology, drawing especially on David Bidney's
recently published "Theoretical Anthropology."
There was a seminar on Robert Redfield's folk-urban
continuum in which I attempted to clarify his great
and little tradition. It seemed to me that this distinc-
tion between a great literary tradition and the tradition of the local uneducated folk was a useful tool for
understanding the dynamics of Islamic societies as
well as other civilizations where the mass of people
were illiterate while a body of written texts inter-
preted by a minority educated class was of central
importance.

LauristonSharp introduced me to Ernst Cassirer's "Essay on Man" which I have always felt was one
of the most important works relating to anthropological theory. As I have noted earlier in these pages,
Cassirer was a neo-Kantian who adapted Kant to
anthropological data.

Morris Opler in a dry and boring style gave us a

valuable and most detailed history of anthropology, the notes from which I have kept and used continually throughout my own teaching career. It is regrettable that Opler never put all his work into print. Opler was a steadfast opponent of Leslie White and his revival of Lewis Henry Morgan's theory of cultural evolution. Biological evolution always appeared to me to be so well established as to be taken as much of a fact as one could get. For one thing no where was there any reasonable alternative explanation for the diversity of life forms. Controversy arose regarding evoution, however, over the mechanisms by which it operated. Some believed that adaptation was the only means through which evolution occurred while others held that while adaptation was extremely important one should not overlook other means as well. (For more detail on this I would refer the reader to the works of Stephen Jay Gould and Richard Lewontin). Cultural evolution as advocated by White and Morgan was a particularly question-able theory. Obviously evolution taken as a very broad and vague concept of change over time and a derivation of forms from other forms was something all anthropologists might agree upon. For several million years the hominid brain has undergone a biological evolution which has included, among other things, a tripling of the brain size. During the course of this evolution humanity achieved increasing sophistication. Biological evolution was paralleled by an evolution of what may be called a proto- culture, finally culminating somewhere between fifty and a hundred thousand years ago in the modern human brain which allowed for the appearance of full fledged human culture.

However, White following Morgan, attempted to place the development of all cultures into a procrustean bed of fixed stages. Each stage was defined in minute detail and each culture was alleged to pass through every stage in lock step fashion. Eventually, it appeared that all would reach the ultimate and glorious heights of civilization which was defined, as someone has said, so that it appeared much like mid-nineteenth century upper New York state (the milieu of Lewis Henry Morgan).

Marx, incidentally, looked with favour on Morgan's theory because, of course, Marx himself wrote of stages within civilization from slavery, to feudalism, to capitalism. Many latter day Marxists held that Russia could not develop socialism because it had never passed through the stage of capitalism and was still feudalistic at the time of the Revolution. Morgan especially appealed to Marx because he stressed the role of property in cultural evolution, but the relation between Morgan and Marx is rather ironic since Morgan was a firm believer in capitalism.

The White-Morgan theory of evolution posed many problems not the least of which was empirical verification. Not all societies are easily placed in one stage or another. They can only be forced into a stage, overlooking much negative evidence. A great many societies seemed to have moved from one stage to another while skipping stages in between. There was an ethnocentric quality to the theory especially in its definition of civilization and apparent belief in the inevitability of human progress.

Faced with these problems White argued that cultural evolution referred to the process of cultural change as a whole and not to the evolution of specific cultures. And to this it was pointed out that if this were the case it would have no scientific significance since it was a case of one and science cannot establish regularities based upon a unique case. At best the White-Morgan evolutionary scheme might possibly describe in a vague fashion - and I would emphasize vague - a parallel evolution of Western-European, Chinese, Indian, Middle Eastern or some Central and South American cultures, but this was only a small part of the whole story. Most Indians of North and South America, the peoples of Australia, the Pacific along with large sections of northern Asia, and much of Africa followed different lines in their histories. Specifically they seemed to have skipped major stages, often being catapulted directly from hunter-gatherers or simple horticulturalists or pastoralists to industrial, iron age society. Cultural change depends upon the history of a group's relationships with others. That is, the evolutionists overlook the role of the diffusion of ideas between peoples. As I learned later, all of these developments are best seen as processes of multilinear rather than unilineal evolution. (see discussion of Juiian Steward's multilinear evolution in the next chapter).

Perhaps fifty years ago there was still a smattering of thinkers who actually believed in the inevitable march of human progress, from the lower to the higher, but it would seem that most have since become rather jaded. One wonders how the ever increasing power and efficiency of the state, the technological developments in warfare, the deliberate destruction of the natural environment, in a word the evolution - the elaboration - of refined methods of killing and torturing can be an upward movement, that is, progress. I think that this discussion of cultural evolution is really about human progress. This is not to deny that there have been here and there remarkable positive movements in human history. One thinks immediately of the developments in modern medicine, of our knowledge of the world around us, or even the decline in capital punishment.

Another problem with White's views was his conception of culture as an entity sui generis, which operated according to its own laws and appeared to be totally independent of all human activity. This was a view which was difficult to accept especially given the fact that all culture was invented, manipulated and determined by humans to begin with.

What I learned most from the study of Talcott Parsons was the major contribution of Max Weber to our understanding of social dynamics. For one thing Weber was a far more perceptive prophet of future events than Karl Marx, the man whom it is said Weber was always attempting to answer. Weber saw the ever increasing movement towards bureaucratization and sophisticated techniques of centralized control in modern society whereas Marx predicted inevitable revolution and the dictatorship of the proletariat - never admitting that this dictatorship would be another form of oppressive rule.

Weber also showed in "The Protestant Ethic and the Spirit of Capitalism" that ideas were important in understanding the causes of social events. Weber attempted to show that capitalism relied in part for its appearance on an appropriate ideology, that for such an economy to develop one had not only to have the necessary organization of the economy and appropriate technology, but you needed a proper world view to motivate individuals. Not all of Weber's data were appropriate, but the principle is important and again is a critique of a Marxist over emphasis upon economic factors such that it smacks of economic determinism.

The department at Cornell lacked a proper number of good lecturers. Robert Smith, who was my advisor, was excellent and by far the best. Lauriston Sharp also did not put you to sleep.

As everyone must know university life is not all books and serious discussion. We had some first class parties. Bernie and Rita Gallin and also Bill Rowe hosted some of the best affairs I have ever attended.

When Jane and I went to Washington, D. C. for summer school she quit her job at the library which had not been too satisfactory anyway. On our return, after my Arabic training at Georgetown, she worked as a secretary in Cornell's Labor School. We had the luck of living and seeking employment in the 50's and 60's when jobs appeared to be plentiful. This is not to suggest, however, that we were in any way prosperous during these years. Every year from 1953 to 1961 we barely got by with an income of about 2800$ and expenses about the same or higher; almost two thirds went for food and rent.

At Cornell we were expected to have two minor fields beside an anthropology major. Most others in the department dealt with this by having an area program as one of the minors and sociology as the other. I was not in an area program so had to select an additional field beside sociology. First, I turned to linguistics and although I have always believed that language is the most important aspect of culture, I have found linguistic analysis boring and difficult. One course I took was a phonemic analysis of Azerbaijani, a Turkic language. I couldn't really get into it. Furthermore the instructor who I had sitting on my doctoral committee, recommended my reading several books in German. The thought of attempting to read this - to me - dry and uninteresting material in academic German was too much.(Cornell incidentally required me to pass examinations in two languages, French and German, and while I passed the French exam I failed in my first attempt at German. "Kitchen" German was always easy, but these extended adjectival constructions in academic German were a real challenge).

I found that while one of my minors was sociology it was still permissible for me to take a second minor in rural sociology since that was a separate department affiliated with the state run part of the university. Rural sociology was more to my liking, although I soon came to realize that in many respects its theory was quite unsophisticated compared to mainline sociology and anthropology. So much of rural sociology's data could be treated as anthropologists do, but the rural sociologists often appeared married to an American model of rural life. Another feature of rural sociology did not appeal to me either. It was strongly oriented to applied work and to training people in agricultural extension, the notion of helping farmers and farmer's wives improve their livelihood. In any event I stayed with rural sociology and sociology as minor fields.

My doctoral committee consisted of Robert J. Smith as chief advisor, Gordon Streib from sociology and Olaf Larson from rural sociology. As I have noted above my original intention was to do a study in Egypt, that is, an ethnographic investigation of an Egyptian village. Initially I thought I might look for specific themes in Egyptian rural culture in line with Morris Opler's theory, but none of this was to be. The political situation especially would prevent such an undertaking. Nevertheless, we had agreed to go to Egypt where I would teach at the American University at Cairo.

In early September, 1956 we sailed on the ocean liner, the Independence, from New York to Naples. We had been provided with second class facilities by the University so the trip was most pleasant. In transit we visited Genoa, Naples and the Isle of Capri. From Naples we sailed on a Turkish ship for Alexandria. This was an especially rough ride particularly through the Straits of Messina where the ship tossed about so that the propeller on the rear end would come out of the water shaking the whole ship. Seasickness was never a problem with me even though my stomach otherwise has never seemed to enjoy what I have given it. When I went down to breakfast the morning following our departure I entered a large dining room and was the only one there to partake of the feta cheese, bread, honey and coffee in the Turkish fashion. Everyone else I was told was sick in bed.

In Alexandria at last, we were met by George Gardiner who took us to a fish dinner by the seaside in Alexandria. What sticks in my mind about this first encounter with Egypt was what seemed to be a large number of wall eyed individuals - the porters on the docks especially. As a poor country Egypt had far more people with eye abnormalities and blindness than I had ever been accustomed to.

In Cairo we were initially put into rooms on the University campus which was directly in the center of the city and across the way from the Nile, the Egyptian Museum and the biggest government building. However, we were hardly settled when the Suez Crisis occurred. Britain, France and Israel all attacked the country in the end of October. I was teaching an evening course when the air raid sirens blew. Some of the girls in the class cried out and I assured everyone it was a practice alert at which point anti aircraft fire drowned out my voice. There were further alarms and gun fire throughout the night and early the following morning. They commenced again in the evening as the British were bombing the Cairo airport. While business seemed to go on as usual in Cairo, the American Embassy, who tend to be alarmist anyway, strongly advised all foreign nationals to leave Egypt. All but one or two of the foreign instructors at the American University decided to evacuate. The faculty was more than half American and this forced the institution to close down until some degree of normality returned. The Egyptian run universities were also closed because of the crisis.

The University officials decided that Geneva would be a good place to wait out the storm. So we packed four suitcases and joined a convoy of vehicles headed for Alexandria and the port of embarkation. As one might expect during such time, rumors of all kinds were rampant. On this trip we passed many people with belongings on the their heads who were leaving their homes in the airport vicinity to go who knew where. At one point we were caught in between the gun fire of three jets and the Egyptian anti-aircraft fire. There were also several hold ups at different check points along the road. On arrival in Alexandria we were caught in another air raid. On the following day we were loaded on a US navy ship and sent to Crete and from there to Naples. The travel by sea took up almost five days in which there was much discussion among the numerous passengers of international affairs, a great deal of rumoring, and standing in line to eat. There was much pressure from the ship operators "to hurry up and wait." The best example of this was the final day when we were to disembark at Naples. We were summarily aroused at 4:30 AM to eat breakfast at five so we could wait around until two in the afternoon to get off. We then proceeded by train to Rome and Geneva. I remained in Geneva for over three months and Jane for still a couple of months thereafter. The main problem was that the United States government took our passports when we left and stamped them as not valid in Egypt so it was impossible for us to reenter Egypt until the stamp was removed. Finally, in early January, 1957 all of us employed by the University were allowed to return before our spouses and families.

While in Switzerland we managed to visit a good part of the country going in late fall and early winter to various mountain domains. The way the Swiss had planted railroads on the sides of mountain cliffs and the cleanliness of the railroad cars was quite impressive. In Geneva I spent some time doing library research for Margaret Read, a British anthropologist who had worked in Africa. I can no longer remember what exactly I was researching, but one embarrassing moment I shall not forget was when I left a note about some problem and addressed it to Dr Margaret Mead who, of course, was, shall we say, a rather notorious and very noted American anthropologist.

On my return to Cairo I recommenced teaching. At this time Cairo was a very bleak place, at least it appeared so to me, since I had to stay in a room on the campus and eat my meals at restaurants. The situation was still unsettled and I was waiting for Jane's return before seriously looking for a more permanent place to live. The long two months wait for the return of University employees' wives from Geneva was filled with one rumor after another, much complaining, and totally incompetent and sometimes callous action on the part of the University administration.

Largely because of the war Egyptians had been whipped up into a peak of nationalistic self glorification. There were greatly exaggerated reports of "the aggression" on Egypt: 40, 000 homes in Port Said destroyed and women and girls raped. School children were taught real blood and gore stories, saber rattling songs and schools were decorated with gaudy and bloody pictures showing the valiant Egyptian army.

Before leaving Cairo in September we had been initiated into the major sights of the city: the Egyptian Museum, the Mohammed Ali mosque, Old Cairo, and the Pyramids. We even had a trip to Ismailiyya and the Suez Canal. It was an odd sight to see huge ships floating along between immense piles of sand. The University planned to make a trip to Luxor during the regular January break. About twenty or so students and half dozen faculty took the train in second class from Cairo to Luxor. Here we spent several days roaming around the desert remains - the Valley of the Kings - and the great temple of Karnak which was the most imposing sight of all. We went on to Edfu to another temple and to the home of one of the students whose family provided all of us with a turkey dinner. It might be noted that Egyptian turkeys are not the huge, fat birds one encounters in North America. Rather they often are

not much bigger than an American hen. Nevertheless, the meal provided was tasty and ample.

In those days the usual teaching load at American
universities was five courses a term and this applied
here as well. For a novice it was an awesome task
to prepare for so many courses and especially where
the students were of a cultural tradition different
from what I had known. I taught courses in both
sociology and anthropology. One of the most enjoyable classes I had was in rural sociology where there
were two mature students who were village dwellers.
From them I learned a great deal about the Egyptian
village. One, especially, lived in a village on the edge
of Cairo and near Giza. He invited me to visit him at
his home on numerous occasions and thus I was able
to become directly acquainted with the village and use
him and his father as "informants." Surreptitiously,
then, I did ethnography. The Egyptian government
refused to permit foreigners to investigate village life
and I believe that policy lasted during most all of
Gamal Abd Al Nasser's regime. I was able to gather
sufficient material to later publish "A Study of an
Egyptian Village" in the journal "Studies in Islam." I
am not sure what it is, but something always attracted
me to the Egyptian countryside. The villages were

always congested and dusty and literally full of shit, but outside there were the fields of cotton and corn, the grazing buffalo, goats and sheep, the date palms, and the Nile as well as perfect sunny weather.

Egyptian students were a most hospitable lot. A few were obsequious, fawning - just plain oily. Many conceived the teacher-student relationship as a kind of game in which they would engage in any number of ways to cheat in examinations and assignments. Later, when I taught at Knox College, there was a practice of having the instructor leave the room in an examination and put all the students on their honour to be honest. Cairo students would have had a good laugh over such an approach. They also are experts at inventing excuses for not doing assignments and are especially good at the "but mine is a special case" argument. One problem that was difficult to deal with was that students sometimes attempted to make gifts to their instructors and this could readily be seen as bribery, although it was often done without any strings attached. Besides being hospitable and outgoing, like other Egyptians they were easy going and had a good sense of humour. Egyptians are always willing to laugh at themselves and not take things too seriously. In this they contrast with Syrians and one can readily understand at least one reason why the union between the two never lasted more than a couple of years.

Students placed an unfortunate emphasis upon memorization, the traditional method of learning. They memorized statements from books which were often meaningless to them. They did not therefore learn how to use what is learned. It was often also difficult to know whether or not a point is understood in a lecture since if asked they all say they understand. If they said they did not understand it would be considered an insult to the teacher. This is a characteristic common to Egyptians: to be polite they will always agree. This is carried further so that if you ask someone where a certain place is or how to get there he will tell you even if he doesn't know.

The American University students were primarily from upper class homes and most were there because they lacked sufficient command of the modern classical Arabic employed in the Egyptian universities. In Arabic there is quite a gulf between how it is spoken on the street and how it is written or spoken in formal situations. Thus, there are three kinds of Arabic: classical which is the seventh century language of the Qur'an; modern classical, an adaptation from the classical and used in all modern writing; and the colloquial speech. The latter varies considerably from one part of the Arab world to another. For example, it is rather difficult for an Egyptian to understand a Moroccan, although because Egypt is the Hollywood of the Arab world, Moroccans have less a problem understanding Egyptians. I have known oriental scholars who on coming to Egypt have gone to the suq(market) and, relying on the Qur'anic Arabic that they have learned, attempt conversations with merchants who have great difficulty trying to understand them.

Many of the students are unfamiliar with the classical language because they are not Arabs. Thus, AUC had a number of Greeks, Armenians and Jews all of whom were Egyptian nationals. Because of the American association some students thought attendance at AUC would provide an easier route to American graduate schools. The vague Christian association of the university brought many Copts (the Coptic Church is the ancient Christian Monophysite church of Egypt allegedly founded by Mark). A few of the students came from embassy personnel. Because of the mixed composition of the student body, perhaps at least half Christian, it was not a representative sample of the Egyptian population as a whole.

Both Jane and I took courses in colloquial Egyptian Arabic. I had had an excellent grounding in the sounds of Arabic phonemes from the Washington experience. Now it was necessary to expand my vocabulary. I have never been that good at learning languages such as the grammar and vocabulary, although I think I am a good mimic of the sound patterns. Indeed, the sounds of different languages have always interested me and I have tended to rank languages as good, bad or indifferent according to whether I like the sounds. Thus at the top of my list as the best sounding language is Italian, but I would put French rather far down that list. Arabic is somewhere in the middle; it is a highly consonantal language and, as a consequence, I always liked hearing English spoken by Arabs because they enunciated every consonant so clearly and distinctly.

Aside from language we took a course on Islamic civilization with Bayard Dodge. I should perhaps remark on an unusual dinner we had at the Dodges. He, having once been president of the American University in Beirut, was familiar with all sorts of noted and elite type people. Therefore, in the course of conversation with others also present at the dinner one heard of references to the American Ambassador to Egypt and to Lebanon, as well as to high positioned people in the State Department, or famous Oriental scholars all by their first names. For us lowly sorts this was all somewhat overwhelming, moving in such influential and "important" circles.

Throughout our stay in Cairo, once we had settled back after the Suez Crisis, we lived in an apartment building owned by one of Egypt's most famous movie stars. We had a one bedroom apartment in the Bab al Luq area near a major market and across the street from a popular mosque. Consequently, we heard very well the call to prayer five times each day and the sermon from the imam at Friday noon. The mosque was so busy they had to block off the street so worshipers could pray there. Also being so close to the market we were in the path of farmers coming with their produce each morning. At five in the morning we could be awakened by the sound of donkeys greeting each other as they carried their loads down the street.

The street was a fascinating place. There were douchers or fights which would erupt between individuals in which the combatants did not seem to be attempting to strike at each other so much as they were trying to tear off one another's shirts or gallibiyyas. In these encounters as well it was always important that they occur only when there were a number of others around who can be counted on to separate the fighters.

The streets were frequented by push cart salesmen. In season they had roast corn available or mangoes. With the latter, men from the nearby office buildings would congregate around the carts eating mangoes and throwing the seeds and skins on the street so that it would become a slippery, slick and slimy mess. Streets were filled with various vendors selling shoe horns, fly swatters, tarbushes. carpets. razor blades, and watch straps among other things. We joked that there were often sellers of pens or writing paper to the illiterate. There were sellers of jasmine, flowers, hardware, clothing, sun glasses and sandals. There were street barbers, beggars and lottery ticket salesmen and pornography peddlers. Aside from all these there were a variety of entertainers including street bands accompanied by dancers, performing mandrels and monkeys, and magicians who allegedly stabbed and cut up victims before your very eyes.

Professional porters and movers are an interesting group. At an early age they start learning to balance heavy objects so that, for example, one man can and does carry a refrigerator on his back up several flights of stairs. One may see three or four men walking down the street, each with a table or sofa balanced on his head. The street was also the site of innumerable coffee shops which were sort of men's clubs where they assembled to smoke the hookah, read a newspaper, or play backgammon in a noisy and tempestuous fashion.

During Ramadan when the fasting hour is supposed to end in the early evening one finds all kinds of people sitting at cafes with food before them waiting for the gun to go off which indicates the end of the fast for the day. Jugs of water are set out on the street for passers by to break their fast. There is heightened activity during the evening as men eat, drink, and smoke at the coffee shops until the early morning hours. In certain sections adjacent to large mosques there is more activity and more of a party atmosphere in various households. During the day one is expected to fast completely and consequently very little is ever accomplished. Everything moves very slowly.

Cairo traffic is a madhouse. Besides having to

watch out for crazy automobile drivers who think the horn is the most important part of a car, there are donkey carts, horse carts, donkey and horse riders, bicycles, motorcycles, , even an occasional water buffalo or camel or sheep and goats. There are pedestrians darting here and there, often with loads on their heads. People often run and hop onto swiftly moving trams or buses, the latter usually so overloaded in the back end that the bus seems almost to scrape along the road.

Across the street from our apartment as well there was a large government building - the Ministry of Waqfs (or Islamic charitable foundations). We had an excellent view of many of the offices and the activity of the employees. It was difficult to determine what, if anything, they did, since each man would come to his office and first thing would sit back and have a prolonged coffee. Then they would each read at least one daily newspaper after which they would gather and have conversations until it was about time for lunch.

We spent considerable time walking around the city, looking at mosques, especially visiting the markets of the Khan Al Khalili and other sights. Once I went visiting old mosques and other Cairo

Islamic antiquities with an Islamic specialist visiting Cairo. We walked here and there until finally I began to realize that I had become the one who was leading us around to the different sights. My alleged guide had been relying on a 15th century map of Cairo and after a bit didn't really know where he was going.

Jane became quite adept at going through the markets and was often asked by the University officials to lead VIP visitors through them. Many of the University employees were Copts and some of them were always eager to expose us to their sub-culture. Therefore, we visited Coptic churches and once went through the entire two hour or more service. Happily this church, probably for tourist purposes, had seats. In the more conservative or typical churches one had to stand for the full period. One thing which struck my Western mind was the casual behaviour of the worshipers which no doubt arose from the fact that the service was so long and in Coptic, a language which few understood. While the service was in progress they often chatted with one another and if one arrived late, even in the middle of the service, he still marched up to the door of the altar and made a full and complete prostration before taking his place in the church.

Once we attended a Coptic baptism with some friends who were having their child baptized. The priest took the child at the baptismal font and, as if he were handling a piece of meat, summarily applied oil and immersed the now screaming baby in the waters of the font. The father had earlier insisted that the water be warmed rather than the apparent usual practice of dumping the young into cold water. Another time we attended a Coptic wedding in which the bride and groom are crowned and placed on thrones while a priest chants on for half hour, as congregants chat amongst themselves.

We went to a couple of old monasteries in the desert northwest of Cairo. One was apparently fifteen hundred years old and has about twenty five monks with a chief who had a degree from Princeton Theological Seminary. The monasteries were not totally accessible by car since one had to walk the final mile and a half through soft sand. They were walled with gardens, rest house, cells for the monks, church, cemetery and bakery inside. The bread which they made was stored and became extremely hard. It was the only food consumed during the forty days of Lent.

We were invited to several different activities

in villages adjacent to Cairo. In one village all the weddings for the year were held at the same time. and during the observation of the death day of the local holy man. While Muslim marriages are civil affairs, there is still much celebration lasting for several days. There is a big parade of the movement of gifts and furniture to the house of the groom. Often joining in are newly circumcised boys riding on horses or camels along with their gifts. Another day involves the parade of the bride to the house of the groom, nowadays in a car, but in the past on camel back, and accompanied by a balady band (One which plays rural music with traditional instruments of pipes and drums). The climax of the affair occurs when the groom arrives and, entering the house, deflowers the bride. The demonstration of a blood stained sheet arouses the crowd of men assembled outside to a pitch of ecstasy as they shout and dance. There is also the usual extensive feasting and the men are entertained with belly dancers. One demonstrates his appreciation for the dancing by stuffing a pound note in the cleavage between the dancer's breasts. Women have their own entertainment in which they dance before each other.

We also engaged in frequent horseback riding.

Near the Pyramids there were individuals who kept a fairly decent string of horses for hire. They were called Arab horses although it is doubtful that they were purebred. In any case these horses were not like those high strung Arabs one frequently finds in the United States. They were gentle, but perfectly willing to give one a good and a fast ride. There were also camels available, but they are slow moving and often not as "cooperative" as horses. Much of our riding was in the desert adjacent to the Pyramids. Once we went with two other couples accompanied by a groom on a desert trip where we slept the night out under the stars. It was all very Hollywood. We also visited interesting rural markets. Many villages have areas for weekly markets in which livestock, vegetables, fruit, pots and pans, clothing and other necessities of village life are available for sale. As strangers to the market we found ourselves followed around by an ever increasing crowd of the curious, much as when we visited other villages. We also rode to large date groves in date picking season. A bare footed picker climbs a tree and fastens a cloth around himself and the tree and drops the picked dates into a basket hanging at his side. When filled the basket is lowered by rope and emptied by a boy on the ground.

It is interesting to note the general ignorance about village life by city dwelling upper and middle class Egyptians, especially amongst the younger people. Not only was their ignorance appalling, but they also did not seem to care at all about the subject. Many felt the peasantry were only a sign of backwardness.

Aside from the immediate vicinity of Cairo we eventually took many trips around the Egyptian Delta. Two or three of the Egyptian teaching staff belonged to families with extensive land holdings in rural parts of the Delta. We were therefore sometimes invited to travel with them to their village. On one occasion we first visited a large mango-orange orchard. Actually it was the first mango orchard ever established in Egypt. Adjacent to it was an azbah, a small village of 3-400 people, originally established by the wealthy landowners to provide labour on their farm. Except for the small population the place is not different from a regular village (Most Egyptian villages have anywhere from three to forty thousand inhabitants). There were the usual mud brick houses with flat rooves upon which were stored corn stalks and manure cakes for fuel. It is said that a villager in Egypt must get used to the odor of cow manure.

Especially is this true for little girls who must collect the manure and make cakes of it for the fire. Some houses also have mud bee hives on their rooves. Aside from storage, rooves are also used as a refuge during summer heat. The houses were meagerly furnished. A mud brick stove in the sleeping quarters had reed mats and mattresses laid out on top of it. One part of the house was used for stabling small animals - goats, sheep, and ducks.

We went for "lunch" at the "manor" house, which was actually two houses. One was of ancient vintage which was a "harem" house with windows in filigree wood. The other house was more frequently occupied. We were seated in the living room with huge gold painted and stuffed chairs after the style of Louis XIV. Then we were invited to dine. Twelve people appeared for the meal which included two turkeys, fish, a pigeon apiece, kufta, veal steak, rice with nuts, raisins and giblets, artichokes in a sauce, potatoes in gravy and desert of kinaffa, milk pudding with coconut, bananas, and oranges. Beer was available throughout the meal and the feast was completed with Arab style coffee - a little Oriental lunch compliments of the pasha landowner. On our trip back to Cairo we were delayed at Benha where a drawbridge was opened to allow the boats (fallukas) to pass through. Some twenty heading south all had full sails and were a spectacular sight while those going north with the current did not need sails.

On other occasions we traveled to the Fayoum region about fifty miles southwest of Cairo to go to a banana plantation. It was eighty acres in which several dozen women were cutting and carrying banana bunches off to a storeroom. Nearby is the village of Basus with about ten thousand people. Houses here like most of those in the Delta are two story affairs to conserve land space for cultivation. (In Upper Egypt houses are often strung out along the desert edge of cultivated land and so have more free room.) We visited the local elementary school which was duly decorated with gaudy and rather crude pictures of the recent battle at Port Said, of modern methods of warfare, the rise of industrialization in Egypt and the crushing of the enemy by Egyptian forces.

We attended several mulids, that is, celebrations of the death day of a holy man. Of course, the Mulid al Nabi, birthday of the prophet, is an immense affair in Cairo with all of the several religious or Sufi brotherhoods setting up tents and performing their rituals. One of the biggest of mulids was that in honor of Sidi Sayyid al Badawi in the city of Tanta, in the Delta. where his tomb is located. While the Nasser regime imposed several restrictions on the activities at the mulid here, there was still an extensive parade of Sufi members; there were several tents set up for the performance of Sufi rituals, especially the zikr, an ecstatic dance. Worshipers entered the tomb to lay their hands upon it and to sacrifice small animals before it. The mulid also had its secular side with amusements including Ferris wheels and displays of all kinds of weird looking people. There was even a stall for circumcision, it being considered a good omen to have one's son circumcised during this occasion. The thousands of visitors camped in tents, out in the open or under bridges.

Other Sufi gatherings were weekly hadras in which the Qur'an and a biography of the brotherhood's founder is recited and a zikr is held. One was for us an exceptional encounter because in order to demonstrate their special devotion to the founder of the order individual participants performed various exercises which we would clearly classify as self torture and were indeed presumably prohibited by the government. One man set fire to a large handful of burning faggots and placed the flames against his bare chest while another heated a sickle in a fire to a red hot condition and proceeded to hold it in his mouth. I could not tell how much either man was burned. Supposedly neither should have been injured because they were protected by the spirit of the founder of the order.

On different occasions we were able to attend a zar. This is a spirit possession cult that is popular among women throughout Egypt. The zar service is led by a shaykha accompanied by men who play instruments. These men incidentally are the only ones present since men in general are not permitted to attend. My presence was permitted because I was a foreigner and so not quite the same as an Egyptian man. The purpose of the gathering is to encourage the spirit (the zar) which is within a woman to express itself and so relieve the woman of the spirit's irritating demands. The music played is aimed at inducing the spirit to speak. The women participants dance and act as well as dress after the fashion of their spirit. In the end there is a sacrifice of a sheep.

During our first year we took an overnight boat with deck passage to Beirut and traveled throughout Lebanon. We went to the archaeological remains at Byblos and Baalbek, then to the Bakaa valley, and northwards to see the few remaining cedars of Lebanon which is called the Switzerland of the Middle East and for good reason. It is quite mountainous and at least until twenty or so years ago was noted as a neutral land in the midst of conflict.

We moved on to western Syria where it appears there are mighty landlords with big estates and large fields of corn, wheat and watermelons. Much of the hill country here is inhabited by Alawites who are a "radical" Shiite sect with some esoteric beliefs and a minority group which has provided many of the most powerful men in the country, including the present ruler. Traveling to Aleppo we encountered villages composed of beehive style houses. In Aleppo there were famous mosques and a citadel. It was about the most interesting city we visited. Aside from the citadel, there are eight miles of covered market with a dazzling variety of little shops where towns people, Kurds, Alawites, Badawin, Gypsies and others all trade. They sell fancy dresses, brass and copper ware, spices, , leather goods of all kinds, vegetables and fruit. Sheep, cow and parts of camel carcasses hang in front of the butcher shops. One has to watch his step going down the narrow streets, particularly the donkeys carrying their big loads or riders. It might be pointed out that most people when thinking of the Middle East seem to envisage camels, when more properly they should think of donkeys which are far more common and widely employed. They have been what largely keeps these places moving and, unlike camels who regularly protest their lot in life, donkeys are placid and patient creatures, often tolerating all kinds of abuse.

Damascus too had its antiquities and large market. At the time of year we were there the oasis of Damascus had large fields of water melons. At the corner of each field was an elevated structure from which watchmen could attempt to insure that no one was stealing water melons. South of Damascus there is a large Druze population, followers of another esoteric religion which was a spin off from Shiism during the eleventh century.

From Syria we passed into Jordan and Palestine. Bus travelers were stopped for hours as inspectors went through all the baggage of every passenger and also studied all of their legal papers. We did not envy them.

The Dead Sea provided an interesting place to attempt to swim. There is so much salt in the water (about 25%) that one can really only float which is quite comfortable, although being summer the water was the temperature of a bath. We were exposed to all the holy sights of Jeruselem. Few of the Christian locations are very appealing, although there was one which claimed to be the true location of the place where Christ was allegedly crucified. It was an attractive garden, esthetically far more pleasing than the official sight at the gaudy and rather disgusting Church of the Nativity. Actually the most pleasing place architecturally was the great mosque of Al Aqsa.

Another trip was more of a major expedition and this was to the Siwa Oasis in the northwestern desert of Egypt. With a half dozen other friends we arranged to go from Cairo to Alexandria and thence to Marsa Matruh on the northwest coast. On the way were the yellowish stone houses of the Awlad Ali, a Badawin tribe which has become largely sedentary and maintains extensive fig orchards which are strung out along side of the road. There are also long sandy beaches. In Mersa Matruh the car which one of our number had acquired for the trip began to have problems. First, the hood was loose and once that was repaired, the engine was shifting its position. Consequently we engaged a man and his large station wagon to drive us to Siwa. At that time nearly the entire distance to the place lacked a road and one had to drive across a desert track. It was important that we have a driver who knew what he was doing and presumably we had our man. We started out having a flat tire about forty miles on the road. After the first fifty or so miles there is no road so one must follow the telephone line. However to avoid periodic drifts of sand the driver inadvertently kept moving further and further away from the line. At last he stopped and we all had to get out and see if we could find the telephone poles. Finally, someone spotted them far off in the distance and so saved the day at least for the time being. But it happened a second time as well. Further, there were places in the sand where we nearly got stuck. There was another problem as well. The back of the van was wide open so that all the dust boiled around us. Someone affixed his jacket to cover the doorway and at the end of the trip it was saturated with dust and sand. One should not be misled, however, into believing the Sahara is all sand dunes. Most of the way to Siwa is an uninteresting flat gravel plain. There are on the route two or three wells which can only be discerned by a pile of dirt which is located beside the well.

We remained in Siwa a couple of days visiting the various parts of the place. It had some historical significance since Alexander the Great is alleged to have visited it. There is a warm spring which provides a soothing experience. Today Siwa is primarily an oasis devoted to olive and date growing. One can walk over the soil and it crunches like hard snow underfoot because of the extremely high salt content. Olives and dates are more tolerant of salt and so prevail here. It is said that they once tried to grow bananas, but they did not survive the saline conditions.

Siwa consists of an old town which is in ruins and beside it is the new town with numerous narrow and winding streets. The town is divided into two distinct parts or moieties. The houses were two or three storied with a courtyard. Some are made of mud, others of salt brick and a few of stone. There is a central square around which are located a few small shops. We were provided lodgings at the government rest house. Food sources were limited; the only meat available was a small piece of camel which we purchased and ground for camelburger. We had found a meat grinder in the guest house, which was good because otherwise the old camel would have been difficult to eat. It wasn't exactly porterhouse steak. One day we had dinner with the mayor of Siwa who for the occasion offered us the heart of a date palm, a considerable honour since in order to provide this, one killed the tree.

Siwans are not Arabs, but Berbers and they represent the eastern most Berber community. The fact that there are isolated Berber communities scattered west of Siwa across North Africa indicates that before the Arab conquest and immigration most all this region was Berber country. The language is quite different from Arabic, but the men anyway are bilingual. Both men and women retain a distinctive dress. The women wear uniquely embroidered pants and blue tobes (robes). Jane enquired about purchasing these and the man soon produced them, not from a store, but from his wife's person.

Our return to Marsa Matruh was even more interesting than our venture out from there. Of course, we had another flat tire. Then, we were a couple of hours from Siwa when the vehicle chugged to a stop. The idiotic driver had sold most of the gasoline in Siwa and just hoped that he might make it home without it or perhaps he didn't care. We were then stuck out in the middle of the Sahara where passing traffic was nearly non existent and with only minimal supplies available. Once a truck carrying Libyans passed and they all had a hearty laugh at out stupid plight. (The Libyan border was not far from where we were). At last some fellows connected with oil exploration came our way and they graciously went off to bring us the necessary gasoline. It was well into the dark of night before we arrived at our destination. Indeed, before arriving at Marsa Matruh we were met by the local police who had come out to look for us. The Siwans were expected to notify the town when anyone was commencing the trip, just as Marsa Matruh was expected to call Siwa when travelers were heading their way. Today, incidentally, I understand that there is a paved road to Siwa and it is frequented by many tourists.

Another January venture was to the Sinai peninsula and the Sinai Monastery. About a half dozen of us rented a vehicle in Suez and one of our party drove once again where there were no roads. Here the way was chiefly through dry wadis (creeks or small river beds) so that the major impediment was large boulders in the way. It was good that there was no rainfall to create floods or we would have been in trouble riding in river beds. We were put up in the

monastery which I understand is the extent of the
Greek Orthodox bishopric of Arabia. There were, as
I recall, less than a dozen monks remaining in the
monastery. They were willing to sell us any amount
of wine, but we provided our own food. Bill Schorger
had suggested we live on tins of corned beef, but Jane,
always the gourmet, had a better idea. She froze beef
steaks and wrapped them well in paper so that we
had a first rate supper. The monastery was extremely
cold; it was, after all, winter and the place was made
of stone and unheated. In addition, it was located
between two high hills so that the sun was available
from about ten to three in the afternoon. One can
understand how the monks acquired the heavy robes
for dress. Because of the cold after supper we all
moved into one bedroom for an evening of conversation. There was a mixture of men and women under
the covers in a bed. We asked for some wine and
I can vividly remember the astonished look on the
monk's face as he entered the room with the wine. He
obviously thought we were all degenerates engaged
in some sex orgy.

In our visit to the monastery we encountered
a small group of Badawin. They apparently are the
only people who frequent the area. To appease the

predominant Muslim population the monks had allowed the construction of a small mosque in the midst of the monastery compound. Aside from the monastery itself and its library which houses very ancient texts, there is Mount Sinai and also the supposed burial place of Aaron to see. And, of course, there are the unending religious services which begin about five in the morning.

One of the advantages of Cairo and the American University was that it was frequented by a continual parade of specialists interested in the general area. At least twice a month there would be some visiting speaker, mostly from the United States. The situation was similar to that in Athens where my daughter later spent some time.

During our years in Cairo it was regularly necessary to transfer money from Egypt to the United States and back and, in the process, alternately change funds from Egyptian pounds to American dollars. Egyptian pounds were always a great deal higher in value at the official rate than at the "real" rate. In addition there were all kinds of Egyptian restrictions on money exchange, so that in order not to lose money it was important to deal very carefully. In practically every letter to my mother in the States there was a request for her to oversee some kind of financial transaction, either my own or for some colleague. As I look back now almost fifty years later it seems that she must have devoted quite a bit of time to these affairs.

Since I was not likely to be able to carry out my research plans in Egypt I began to look for alternatives. It so happened that Sa'ad Ad Din Fawzi, vice-chancellor of the University of Khartoum, was visiting the American University and I talked to him. He was most enthusiastic about the possibility of my coming to the Sudan and promised much help. The American University also agreed that for the remaining six months of my contract I could be relieved of teaching and other university responsibilities to go the Sudan. I would also have a small grant from the Social Research Center at the university - money that was originally from the Ford Foundation - rather ironic since it was that institution that had rejected my original application for funds. As a result we made plans to visit the Sudan on the winter holiday to assess the situation.

We then made a trip via Sudan Airways which at that time ran a small plane that seated about forty passengers to Wadi Halfa where it stopped for lunch and then proceeded to Khartoum. I recall the meal well. It consisted of a plate of boiled cauliflower. In Khartoum we were received with great hospitality and assured of an initial place to say when we arrived for the more prolonged visit.

Leaving Cairo was some disappointment. We had had such an enormously rich, fulfilling and enjoyable two and a half years there. For me it was never surpassed; the people, the activities, the stimulation - one should be so fortunate.

We left Cairo in January, 1959. I wanted to have a further look at the countryside as we traveled, so we took the train from Cairo to below Aswan where the Egyptian railroad ended. From there the trip was by boat up the Nile to Wadi Halfa. The boat trip allowed us to see Abu Simbol, the great ancient Egyptian monument to Ramses which was later removed to higher ground to avoid flooding by the creation of Lake Nasser. The boat trip was both pleasant and rather unusual in that we proceeded in all this Nile water while on either side of us were low lying parched, brown and lifeless hillocks. On arrival in Wadi Halfa we boarded the Sudan rail for Khartoum. The rail followed the Nile a short distance before making a short cut across the desert to Abu Hamed when it again followed close to the river and where one passes numerous villages. This railroad incidentally was the first and one of the rare modern 'improvements" introduced by the British during their control of the Sudan. Of course, the rationale for building it was not to aid the Sudanese so much as to give the British better control of the place. A similar railroad was constructed to Port Sudan, but in that case the motivation was more to ease the transportation of cotton out of the Sudan to the British mills. When we visited Khartoum some twenty years later we enquired about the rail service between Khartoum and Egypt. We were told that there was now only one train a week and it could not be counted on to run even then. Further it no longer provided any sleeping quarters or dining facilities.

At Khartoum we put up at the Pink Palace. This was used by the University of Khartoum to provide for university visitors. It was hardly a palace, although it may have been thought as such because Haile Selassie, the Emperor of Ethiopia, took up temporary residence here when he fled the Italian invasion in the late thirties. Furthermore, it was for the Sudan a large house and had indoor plumbing. Most of the sewerage in Khartoum was disposed of by pit latrines and by outhouses supplied with heavy lead buckets which were emptied each evening by men, all of whom were from the Nuba Mountains southwest of Khartoum. They took the buckets on their heads and dumped the contents into "honey" wagons which carried the waste off.

We lived for a few months in. a small house adjoining the Pink Palace. Later we were able to rent a new house built for government employees which was assigned to Andreas and Waltraud Kronenberg who were at the time engaged in anthropological research in the southern Sudan. This housing showed many signs of defective construction. The cement used had such a high content of sand that it became filled with tiny vermin. During the brief rainy season in June and July the water leaked through the roof and when the lights were turned on this caused a great crackling of electricity. Another general problem of living in Khartoum was the haboob season when winds carried the silt from the Gezira region south of Khartoum in storms which made the skies black and forced one to shut all the windows and doors, which was to no avail since the silt seeped through into the house covering everything. In addition, of course, closing all the windows raised the temperature in the house precipitously. Actually, the worst time of year in Khartoum was the month of May when temperatures regularly got up to 115 Fahrenheit and, of course, there was no air conditioning or any other artificial relief from the oven like heat. Those few who had refrigerators tended to fill them with jugs of water

My immediate need was to select a village to study and obtain government permission to do so. However, here again a major problem arose. As when we went to Egypt our plans were interrupted by the Suez Crisis, so in Sudan our plans were interrupted by a political crisis of a slightly different sort. For two years the Sudan had operated as a parliamentary democracy. A coup d'etat turned it into a military dictatorship under General Ibrahim Abboud at the end of 1958 just a few weeks before our arrival. Sa'ad Ad Din Fawzi had promised no problems in undertaking research. But he did not know how the Abboud regime would react to such an idea. It declared that I could do research in any village of my choice so long as I spent every night in Khartoum. The reasoning for such a limitation was difficult to fathom. It certainly placed severe restrictions on where I might go and how I might proceed.

Muhammad Umar Bashir, the University secretary, was most helpful. He suggested the nearby village of Buurri al Lamaab, not only because it was very close to Khartoum, but also because it was a distinct community with an interesting Sufi organization headquartered there. The situation looked interesting, although I would have preferred a more agriculturally oriented community and one not so highly adapted to modern and urban ways. Thus, I began my affair with Buurri al Lamaab.

Perhaps I should point out to those not familiar with this area that, except for the far north, the northern Sudan along the Nile is an Arab enclave. While at best only half the population of Sudan is Arabic speaking, it is they who are the politically and economically dominant part of the population. Sudanese Arab culture also differs in several respects from that of Egypt and there has been some ambivalence towards Egyptians by the Sudanese Arabs and other ethnic groups in the country. This attitude derives from the 19th century rule of the Sudan by the Egyptians, also from the fact that Egypt is a much more powerful neighbor and one which controls most of the Nile water.

The village of Buurri al Lamaab has similarities

to others along the northern part of the Blue Nile. The houses are primarily of mud brick surrounded by walls, some of which have pieces of glass inserted on the tops of the walls to prevent undesirables from trying climb over them. A few residences were made of fired brick. The village stands adjacent to cultivated land on the river side and contains innumerable twisting alley ways. It was established in the latter part of the 19th century by two extended families and gradually grew with an influx of outsiders because of the nearness to Khartoum. Following the First World War Sharif al Hindi, a major Sufi leader, established his headquarters in the village and this drew further immigrants. Thus, the village acquired a rather mixed population. The name Lamaab suggests a collection of differing peoples and indicates a traditional Sudanese practice of attempting to bring peoples of differing backgrounds together in a myth of kinship. Probably at a much earlier time the Lamaab people would eventually come to consider themselves as a separate tribe or at least a clan, but its creation occurred too late in time for this process to develop properly. Thus, many in the village identified themselves as Lamaabiyyiin, implying that they were all members of the same tribe descended from a common ancestor which, of course, was not so. They all also retained their own lineage affiliation.

I began visiting Buurri in early March with the temperatures now going towards 100 degrees Fahrenheit during the day. There were few people around given the midday heat and the fact that so many worked in Khartoum. I chatted a bit with a local shop keeper and a couple of younger fellows who were cultivating vegetables in fields along the riverbank. My Cairene Arabic was not very good, but they seemed to understand me better than I could them in their northern Sudanese dialect. Shortly, I came into contact with a couple of young men who lived in the village and spoke a bit of English. They introduced me to one of the local notables and arranged for me to talk to the 'umda (mayor). The latter interview I found extremely difficult since I could hardly understand a word the mayor said. Occasionally, I had the assistance of a university student who lived in Khartoum, although he proved quite unreliable when it came to keeping appointments.

After some three weeks of aimless wandering, my previous acquaintances introduced me to 'Abdallahi Muhammad Al Haj Babikr who proved to be the answer to my dreams. He was the sort of person who seemed to know everything and could make any kind of arrangement, as well as have the time and interest to devote to the project. It was fortunate that when I told villagers I was interested in their history they understood history pretty much as genealogy and kinship relationships which is exactly what I wanted. 'Abdallahi had made this subject his life enterprise. He worked in Khartoum as a labourer for the Sudan Light and Power, had a wife and five children. He was born in Buurri forty three years before and was descended from original founders of the community. He had worked for the British during their occupation of the Sudan and like many other Sudanese had a strange high regard for them. Beside his great interest in local village affairs and relationships, his attraction to things British was another motivation for being interested in talking with me at great length. He always called me Barclays because the bank was Barclay's.

To start with, 'Abdallahi suggested that we walk around the village going from house to house and learning something about each resident. He already knew everyone by name and most of their business and, of course, what I dearly required was someone well known and at least tolerated in the community who could introduce me to others and so be received with some confidence. Through this process I eventually acquired from the residents everyone's name, family composition, kin ties, as well as an idea of the socio-economic status by the sort of dwelling they had and their occupation.

I soon learned as well that 'Abdallahi was recognized as a kind of genealogical expert in the village. Several times I recall that we would be talking to an informant in which 'Abdallahi would say something to the effect that so and so was the informant's father's mother's sister's son and the informant would say no, to which 'Abdallahi responded by going through the names of all the relatives pointing out the informants error. It was a matter of great luck to be awarded such assistance - the true key informant and authority on village affairs - but one had to be careful about too quickly coming to accept everything he said at face value and I'm afraid that I too often fell into this trap.

'Abdallahi was not a religious man. Although he fasted Ramadan like everyone else, he never went to the mosque, never prayed and did not belong to any religious brotherhood. It was necessary to obtain information pertaining to religion and other beliefs from other sources and other means. I talked with the head of the Hindiyya tariqa, the Sufi brotherhood which more or less dominated most of the village, and with the imam, the prayer leader of the village mosque, and attended various and sundry religious affairs. The women, especially the elderly, were familiar with the numerous and complex rituals which were observed in connection weddings and similar affairs. They were the masters of the popular culture while the men mastered the Islamic tradition. Consequently it would have been difficult for me to obtain much information on the popular culture given the social division in this society between men and women. Eventually Jane was able to collect a considerable amount of data from the women for my research.

Another person who was of immense help to me was 'Abd Al Rahim Ahmad Bilaal. He was quite a bit older than 'Abdallahi and could read and write, whereas 'Abdallahi was illiterate. He had traveled widely for one from Buurri al Lamaab. In his youth he had joined the British merchant marine. Now he was an employee of an irrigation company. He had reared a family and was already a grandfather. While he was born and raised in the village he was no where near as conversant with its affairs as 'Abdallahi, but he assisted me in many ways. He belonged to the Cultural Club and introduced me to it. Cultural and sports clubs had become popular in the Sudan by this time and were places where men gathered in the evening to talk, drink tea, and, where they were available, play various games or watch a moving picture. Once I offered an English class which began with a dozen, but after a few meetings had declined to two or three.

Eventually, we were invited to weddings and other ceremonies. Unlike Egyptian and other Middle Eastern marriages there is no climax involving the demonstration of the bloody sheet as proof of the virginity of the bride. This is because women almost universally are subjected to the operation of infibulation where the vulva except for a small hole is almost completely sewn together. Often penetration is impossible without first resorting to a midwife to enlarge the opening surgically, a practice often necessary after a marriage.

One of the features of weddings included a gathering of adult men for a drinking party. Each man was seated against the walls of the room. One man carrying a kerosene tin of liquor and another a glass moved from one person to the next pouring out a drink which was to be quickly consumed. They proceeded around the room several times. There was little or no conversation and all was carried out in a very sober and dour fashion. The liquor was a distilled date wine which I thought did not have a very good flavour; it was certainly strong enough. In Egypt Sudanese had a reputation as drunkards or at least as heavy imbibers of strong drink. In the Sudan Egyptians had a reputation for being heavy smokers of hashish. It is true that Sudanese probably do consume more alcohol than other Muslims. Throughout much of the Arab Sudan, villages have houses marked by white flags where one can drink beer that has been made in some local person's house. With the prevailing fundamentalist regime in the present Sudan such places may no longer exist.

After a burial it was customary to hold evening meetings for Qur'an recitation in honour of the deceased. While it may sound rather macabre such gatherings were important, since one could count on everyone in the village being in attendance at least part of the time.

I sometimes went out onto the river banks to talk with farmers. It is interesting to note that in Egypt an ordinary dirt farmer is a peasant (fallah) while in the Sudan he is a 'cultivator' (muzar'ah), a more dignified term. In the northern Sudan river bank agriculture is most common, but there are also islands in the Nile which are commonly cultivated because during the periods of the high Nile in early fall these places are flooded and, thus, irrigated with a minimum of effort. Buurri farmers exploited Kulkula, a small island, for vegetable production.

In late November, 'Abdallahi invited us to accompany him to the Gezira. This is the main agricultural area of the Sudan where the major export crop, cotton, is grown. 'Abdallahi had a close relative, his mother's brother, who lived in Burtabayl village in the midst of the Gezira and about fifteen miles from the city of Wad Medani. 'Abdallahi did not want to take the train because he was afraid that he would be forced to go into the fourth class carriage while we would go second class. Thus, we journeyed on the classless bus instead. There was at this time no road to Wad Medani, our destination. The trip would be across country on rough tracks.

Abdallahi's relative was an important member of the community and extremely well off by Sudanese standards. The government granted individuals land holdings or tenancies which were supplied water by a massive irrigation scheme originally developed by the British. However, it was possible to obtain control over several tenancies by a bit of finagling. One might register for a tenancy under a son's name or a wife's. At one time it was apparently possible to buy tenancies from current holders. With an accumulation of tenancies one soon required hired labour and this was made readily available by the West African population, composed of would be pilgrims on route to Mecca. The West Africans would work their way across the continent. Most of them seem never to achieve their goal, settling in villages they created adjacent to Arab Sudanese ones. They could not qualify for any tenancy themselves since they were not Sudanese, but they did provide a labour force for tenancy owners.

'Abdallahi 's kinman not only had income from several tenancies, but also from two tractors he owned and employed drivers to hire out for plowing and cultivating. His house was the largest in the village, had piped water, even a shower (which a bunch of frogs seemed also to enjoy), and best of all, a gas operated refrigerator. But the uncle would not run the refrigerator in winter (From late November until

February temperatures could sometimes descend to as low as 50 Fahrenheit at night). He did not see the need for one in the "cold' weather. Before going to bed we were always brought a bowl of frothy milk to drink. The practice was to put sugar in the bottom of the milk pail and milk the cow very rapidly so a sugary froth appeared.

On our return to Khartoum the bus as usual ran along a rough pathway and it soon became dark. All of a sudden it began to jerk from side to side as if running over a continual pile of high boulders. On coming to a stop we found that we were in the midst of a flock of sheep and what felt like boulders were actually sheep. Before proceeding it was necessary to count all the dozens of dead sheep so the poor shepherd might seek some kind of compensation.

Another trip we took to Port Sudan via Gedaraf and Kassala by train. We stopped first at Kassala and the next day expected to board a train for Port Sudan which was supposed to arrive at 10 AM. We duly arrived at the station to await the train. Finally, after seven hours it ambled into the station. It was said that some woman had fallen off the train and this caused the delay. We were scheduled to stop off at Sinkat before Port Sudan which, if the train arrived at a reasonable time, would have got us there in daylight. As it was we arrived closer to midnight in pitch darkness. Sinkat is a tiny station in the Red Sea Hills and had no lights anywhere. Happily we were met and taken to a government rest house for our overnight stay.

The next day we were escorted around the area by a most cordial local district commissioner (At this time the Sudanese still retained the British administrative system). We enjoyed a coffee ritual with the local Hadendowa elders, Hadendowa being a branch of the Beja ethnic group which inhabit the Red Sea Hills region. The geography and flora of this area were the most interesting of any part of the Sudan we visited, for here were numerous hills covered with succulents of the genus Euphorbia: great needle-less cactus type trees twelve to fifteen feet high.

In a recent report on the Sudan I read that the Sudan is " a big, bad and dirty place." While this was written, obviously to note the current oppressive regime in the country, it is still not quite true. Certainly most of the northern Sudan would have little attraction for tourists except for these hills. It may be dusty or sandy, but it certainly is not dirty. And this statement overlooks the character and nature of the people who live here. They may be poor, but they are a kindly and hospitable people with a great sense of humour.

We finally came to Port Sudan and visited from there the old Turkish town of Suakin where the apartment like residences have been long since abandoned. On returning to Port Sudan the driver stopped periodically to pick up men who had been fishing for the day on the Red Sea. The fish, having been sitting for hours in the sun, were beginning to get a little ripe and this combined with the somewhat rancid butter that the Beja tribesmen plastered in their hair produced an interesting odour for a good part of our trip.

Once a friend in Buurri al Lamaab invited us to come with him to his mother's village on the other side of the Nile. It was called Umm Dubaan, meaning mother of flies. I do not remember it as having many flies so much as there were tiny biting insects the Sudanese called nimitti and they certainly disturbed our sleep for an entire night.

Umm Dubaan was a centre for a Sufi religious brotherhood and a local madrasa or Qur'anic school. Our visit occurred during a commemoration of the founder of the brotherhood in which there were religious exercises for a full night including hymn singing and the Sufi "dance" or zikr. The Qur'anic school disciplined its students in the most Medieval fashion. Boys walked about with shackles on their legs either as punishment for some misdemeanor or to prevent them from running away.

For practically all of my contacts in the Sudan I was limited to the company of men. I could only speak to a woman after long acquaintance with her male kin and only in the most formal circumstances. If it had not been for Jane's assistance there would have been much material that I would not have been able to access. A single man in an attempt to study such a culture would essentially be able to obtain only half of it. For Muslim societies it is best to have a couple and, preferably one with children. We were sometimes accosted with the question: "What! You've been married six years and have no children yet?" A single woman would have more success than a single man since she can gain easy access to the female world and to a considerable extent be accepted as a female "male" in men's circles.

During my field work in the Sudan I made innumerable errors especially of etiquette. Once in the early stage of my visits to Buurri I was taken to a gathering of a returned Meccan pilgrim - the kind of gathering I had already been exposed to several times. I blurted out within hearing distance of the host: "Why have I been taken to this place?"

It was customary to visit the house and family of a person at the time of his death and on entering to approach the chief mourners to raise one's hands and recite Al Fatihah, the prayer which opens the Qur'an. Since I found nothing disagreeable with the prayer - it is one which could be recited by Christian or Jew as well as Muslim - I followed along with others and stood before the mourners reciting the Fatihah. This annoyed some of the other guests - that a non-Muslims should recite this prayer. I did not repeat this faux pas.

I am reminded of a report recorded in one of the Case Studies in Anthropology of an anthropologist who went to a Muslim village in West Africa and proceeded to participate in all the Muslim rituals including the five daily prayers (salat). Because these case studies are widely used to teach students about what anthropologists do I wrote to the publishers protesting this what seemed highly improper behavior. These prayers are Muslim specific. That is, no one would recite them unless he was a Muslim believer since among other things they proclaim Muhammad the prophet of god. I felt that this anthropologist was clearly engaging in deceit since he was not a Muslim and was only indulging in these rituals to attempt to build rapport.

Once, late in my stay, I was running short of funds and when I took pictures of a man and his family I asked to be paid for the cost of copies for him. This was really gross. One does not ask for remuneration for such things.

In March we planned to leave the Sudan for home. I had sent off a number of letters to various universities inquiring about the possibility of obtaining a teaching position, but being so far from North America was not conducive to arousing any interest from any university. We thus returned to the United States with no idea where we would be going next. Bidding farewell to 'Abdallahi and Abd Al Rahim especially was difficult. They both had been so good and yet I felt that there was such a distance between us. Further, I was the one who was advantaged in this enterprise. What glory was in it for them?

My parents had moved from Newton to Falmouth on Cape Cod and there I spent a few months writing up my notes and preparing the thesis. My mother, seeing that I was just spending my time writing, and without compensation, thought I should go down to the local Safeway and get a temporary job bagging and carrying out groceries! In due course, I did have a couple of offers for university employment, finally accepting a position as Assistant Professor at Knox College in Galesburg, Illinois.

CHAPTER IV

Launching a Career and a Family

Knox College was one of those institutions which considered itself somewhat better than it was. I think the administrators felt it was a Harvard of the Midwest. At other universities it was alleged that the motto was 'publish or perish'. At Knox College that motto was modified to ' publish and perish'. Your interest and work were to be directed to and for the students alone. You were to go to your office in the morning and remain there with your door open to invite any passing student in for a chat, except where you were engaged in teaching a class, or over in the Gizmo, the college cafeteria, sitting around shooting the bull with students. Saturday night, if I recall correctly, one should be in the gym rah rahing for the college basketball team. To devote time to publishing and research was not really approved. Particularly, it was a gross error if you dared publish as much or more than your department chairman - which invariably meant nothing at all. As an instructor your job was to acquire the PhD, the sacred emblem of professorialism, and then to forget about research, just paying attention to student needs (I almost wrote "just baby sitting the kiddies ", but thought that was a little too nasty).

Knox had a habit of hiring a good number of competent people. Then, within two to three years they would be fired or they would leave on their own accord, so that there would always be left, providing continuity, the same basic core of old fools.

I had not before experienced the US Middlewest, but it now seemed a very narrow-minded and insular part of the world. Knox had a bare handful of individuals classified as foreign students, two of whom were from Hawai'i! Cairo, Egypt was pronounced Cayro and Cornell referred to Cornell College, a small institution in Iowa. Veteran staff members conceived of themselves as Renaissance men when they were mere dilettantes.

The city of Galesburg was drab and uninteresting. The winters were as snowy and cold as the summers were unbearably hot and sticky. We lived in a second floor one bedroom apartment in a house owned by the college. It was barely a step or two above our accommodations at Cornell. Among other things the heating system was old and dilapidated. In winter the radiators banged and clanked and finally the whole business exploded such that the house was practically knocked off its foundation. We spent weeks in a local hotel until repairs were completed. All of this was a great embarrassment to the college - that they would be the owners of such a place.

One of the cultural features of Galesburg and Knox that I found difficult to fathom was the inordinate interest in the Civil War. Apparently Abraham Lincoln had one of his debates with Douglas on the campus. It almost seemed that the world turned on the Civil War. The not very impressive library had, in relation to its total number of volumes, an enormous collection of Civil War material. It was all just another indication of the narrow, ethnocentric orientation of the college.

Despite the adverse features of Knox and the Midwestern milieu my stay there was highly productive and in many respects quite enjoyable, the latter because of the good fellowship of some of the lower echelon staff.(all of whom, like myself, eventually left for better pastures). Then, both of my children were conceived in Galesburg (which we tended to pronounce with a soft 'g', as Knox finally became knoxious).

Alan was born in 1961 and Alison in Eugene, Oregon in 1963. I don't believe that I would get very high grades as a father, although I have been impressed with how they "turned out," especially compared to what I have heard about other people's children. I would say, however, that over the years, and for many years after they reached their majority, I have subsidized their incomes with several tens of thousands of dollars and they seemed to take it too much for granted. In any case in my opinion they have been a success and I would say that is at least partially due to Jane and to a household which was not always in constant turmoil. Perhaps also good genes are somehow involved. I do believe, however, that I have at least impressed upon my children the value of education and learning and of knowledge. I have taught the need for a skeptical outlook. As well, I have tried to help develop in them a social conscience and concern for their fellow humans. I am grateful that I see all of these features in both my children.

Children from the parental point of view are, I believe, at their best and most interesting when they are anywhere between age one and seven. We have the most problems when they reach puberty and pass through the teens. Obviously, the problem here is the increasing independence and search for independence coupled with the fact that apparently the mind is not fully matured until one enters the twenties. Nevertheless, I do not recollect any difficulties with our children during this period; the most difficult time for Alison - or for her parents - seemed to be when she was about one and two years old when she was given to having tantrums.

During my stay at Knox I read two books which greatly influenced me: Ralf Dahrendorf's "Class and Class Conflict in Industrial Society" and Julian Steward's "Theory of Cultural Change." Dahrendorf presents an excellent critique of Marx and tried to point to a social theory which integrated structural functionalism and conflict theory. Functionalism holds that the several elements which make up a society all make a contribution to its operation so that it is an integrated, harmonious whole. Any conflict which arises in such a system must be the result of some external influences. Thus, in studying cultural change functionalists were primarily interested in the process of acculturation in which one culture was being exposed to massive influences from another such as the Amerindian contact with the Europeans.

Conflict theory holds that dysfunctions and conflict may be generated within any social system as a result of internal contradictions arising within it. Thus, change may occur as a consequence of external factors or internal ones. Marx had based his theory on conflict, but he laid an excessive emphasis on economic factors and overlooked the role of pure power as a device which generated resentment and conflict. Capitalism, as Marx said, generated a conflict between capital and labour. But that is only one source of conflict, for in any complex social system conflict arises from the drive for power by bureaucrats or managers, military leaders, or technicians.

Dahrendorf, then, proposed a social theory which recognizes that society tends to be an integrated whole where the various elements do function, but that at the same time internal contradictions arise within the system that provoke conflict and thus change.

Steward's book argued that cultural evolution was the search for regularities in the process of cultural change. Several cultures that shared regularities comprised one line of evolution, but there were others as well so that one had a multilinear evolution of cultures. In biological evolution there was no unilineal process, but rather there was diversification towards a number of different forms over time. There were lines of evolutionary change. For me, this multilinear evolution, whether cultural or biological, did not have any particular direction. The change was not onward and upward - progress - rather it was just change - blind change.

Much earlier I had thought Albert Schweitzer was an important thinker who practiced what he preached. I came to realize that he had a quaint racism in which Africans were little children who required the guidance of the mature and knowledgeable Europeans. However, I continued to be impressed by his "Philosophy of Civilization "and, even more so by his doctrine of reverence for life.

Three major incidents occurred in 1961. The first was the birth of our son, Alan. He was born with club feet and had to have casts put on his feet. One could always tell when he was awake because of the clacking sound made by the casts as he moved his feet. I always found his earliest years the most enjoyable to observe and participate in, although I am not certain that Jane always thought so.

The second major accomplishment of that year was the completion of the PhD thesis and receiving the degree, although I did not actually go to Cornell to accept it. Thirdly, we acquired television. I have always been slow to adopt new technology. We had a radio, and I recollect spending many an hour in the evening listening to it when we were at Cornell, the broadcasts of the McCarthy hearings being a most memorable event. It was not until we went to Cairo that we adopted a record player. We had no typewriter until we went to Cornell and no television until long after everyone else had one. Our first car was purchased in 1963 and a computer was not introduced until 2001.

While at Knox I began to develop a collection of music records which very much later became a collection of disks. I never cared for so-called popular music and always preferred what is called classical music. I liked best those composers who were the noisiest. Thus, my favorite has always been Beethoven and some of Wagner, Sibelius and Bruckner. As well I found Schumann and Haydn stimulating. Eventually I was introduced to Telemann and Stozell, although my preferences have been for symphonic pieces. It has always been interesting to me that one may find great pleasure in music composed by individuals whose ideology and way of life is so contradictory to one's own. For me, numerous works with a deeply religious intent are so satisfying while I have no use, intellectually, for that intent. Military music is another case in point. I have a disk of the martial music of the Ottoman Turkish empire which I enjoy. That which plays to the emotions is an entirely different sphere from the intellectual and fully rational.

As I have already intimated Knox College was not exactly my cup of tea. Thus, in 1963 I was casting around for another location and was accepted at the University of Oregon. I had, of course, been in Oregon before when I was in the objectors camp during the war. Oregon not only had a physical attraction, but it was less given to the militarism and yokelism prevalent in American society. Oregonians were a conservative lot but they, nevertheless, seemed more tolerant and were an improvement over Middle Westerners.

Soon after our arrival in Oregon our daughter, Alison, was born. About the same time I was asked to prepare my PhD thesis for publication at Cornell

University Press. The thesis entitled " An Ethnographic Study of a Suburban Village in the Sudan" was published as "Buurri al Lamaab: A Suburban Village in the Sudan" in 1964.

The University of Oregon was the first place I taught which was not largely composed of rich kids. Cornell, the American University at Cairo, and Knox were all primarily institutions for the upper class. But in actual fact I never noticed much difference in terms of academic ability because of class differences.

At Oregon I was in a department where I was in the company of a few anthropological notables, e.g., Homer Barnett, Luther Cressman and Albert Spaulding and they proved to be the most congenial of colleagues. The teaching load was less than at Knox, a reflection of the recognition of the significance of research and also of the role of a graduate degree program. I taught a course on Primitive Societies - a term I did not like because it seemed pejorative - and also one on the people of the Middle East. I directed a couple of BA honours theses and supervised a PhD candidate.

Graduate students were required to take qualifying examinations and faculty were asked to contribute questions for these. David Aberle, a supporter of Leslie White's theory of cultural evolution, was given the job of selecting appropriate questions. One I submitted, with tongue in cheek, asked for comment on the statement by David Bidney that Lesilie White' s concept of culture was a form of animism. Aberle did not include the question in the examination.

The country was becoming more embroiled in the hostilities in Vietnam and we were led down the garden path by Lyndon Johnson whose campaign made him the "peace"candidate and portrayed Goldwater as the epitome of war mongering in the 1964 election. Primarily from fear of Goldwater, we voted for the first and only time and backed Johnson. It seems to me that American voters in 2004 might well consider the election of 1964 when we were all stampeded into supporting Johnson because he was allegedly so much superior to Goldwater when there was no difference. So today one should not be stampeded into voting for Kerry because he seems to be superior to Bush when in fact there is no difference.

We soon joined with others to form an anti-war group. The following year David Aberle was instrumental in organizing a "teach-in" in which we participated.

That summer I was invited by Walter Lehn, director of the Middle Eastern program at the University of Texas, to teach a couple of courses on the area. I made the foolish mistake of merely informing the department chairman that I was going to Texas for the summer and the fall terms, rather than asking his permission. I apologized for my error and, receiving his blessing, proceeded to Texas.

At Texas we lived next to an Episcopalian minister who had been a Roman Catholic priest. For years he had carried on a double life as a practicing Catholic priest, while living with a woman who was a nun and who, during this clandestine period, had given him several children. Eventually, I gather his conscience prevailed and he gave up the double existence and changed his denominational affiliation. One of his many children was about Alan's age and for the first time Alan found immense pleasure in a playmate.

Austin, the location of the University, was a rather pleasant town at that time, although it seems that it has now become a major metropolis. There were parks with pecan trees which provided nuts. We often visited one of several swimming pools. During the day in summer one could roam the residential districts and never see a living thing, except the occasional maid walking to work. Everyone else was shut up in an air conditioned world. One member of the anthropology department, however, had no air conditioning., but he was a born and bred Texan and his house was built in that Southern fashion so that windows and doors were arranged to maximize any breeze.

Probably our most memorable activity in Texas was a trip to Mexico where we journeyed to Saltillo and Monterey. Some of the Mexican villages reminded me of those in Egypt except that there were quite a few pigs running around.

After Christmas we returned to Oregon. We now lived fifty miles from the Pacific Ocean in the west and fifty miles from the mountains to the east and a little further to the more arid regions of central and eastern Oregon. Thus, one had access to all kinds of ecological zones. To me the most attractive was the yellow pine country of central Oregon, especially around Redmond, where we traveled frequently. The coast was also of interest and we sometimes went to the beach, ducking down behind big logs to avoid the wind and lighting large fires during the colder months. The main problem was that the ocean water was so bitterly cold it made swimming impossible. Sometimes the Oregon weather left something to be desired. This was especially true in winter when weeks could pass with no sun. Our first summer there was so overcast and cool tomatoes in our garden never ripened.

I was becoming particularly disturbed by the Vietnam war and annoyed at having to pay taxes to support it. In addition, the University of Oregon seemed to think that one should accept living in such beautiful surroundings as part of his salary. Indeed, the University had invented interesting devices which essentially cheated the employee. They withheld payment of one's salary for the three summer months until September and so earned the interest from the money. They also withheld a small part of the salary for a pension plan, but if one left the university they returned only the principle and kept the accumulated interest. By these practices they no doubt made a few hundred thousand dollars a year from their employees.

Finally, I decided to leave Oregon and go to a Canadian university. I found an opening at the University of Alberta in part through the assistance of Gordon Hirabayashi whom I had known at the American University at Cairo and was now chairman of Alberta's Sociology Department. Before moving to Alberta, however, I was asked to teach a summer course at the University of California at Berkeley. This was a most stimulating place. The bookstores on Berkeley's main street were more than impressive. We participated in demonstrations against the Vietnam War and on one occasion joined a huge march in San Francisco. We found ourselves directly in front of a large band of Trotskyites and I was concerned about not being identified with them.

My appointment at Alberta was at the associate professor level and at this time Alberta had more funds available so that it could be more generous than many other institutions. This, however, changed in due course. For the first time we purchased a house and it was within walking distance of the university. Eventually we learned that we had another advantage as well in our choice of residence and that was in our neighbours. Mac and Olive Elofson were the best neighbours we've ever had as well as good friends.

Our first year in Edmonton was uneventful. Members of the anthropology department did not appear much interested in us and we did not find some of them appealing. The department had been newly organized and separated from sociology and still only offered a bachelor's degree. Charles Brant was the chairman and qualified for a sabbatical leave in 1967. He was the first anthropologist employed at Alberta having been there since 1961. There was opposition by the administration to his taking the sabbatical since the department had just been created and there appeared to be no feasible candidates for acting chairman to replace him. Of the remaining six members I was the senior and I suppose, therefore, by a process of elimination, Brant approached me to take on the job, arguing that if I didn't do so he would be deprived of a sabbatical. Reluctantly, I agreed. After all, I hardly knew anything about the university and its workings and I had no taste for administrative work.

Many people seem to believe that the chairman is some prestigious and high status position worthy of great respect. This is not so. The chairman is a bureaucrat and must waste his time on many a frivolous exercise at the expense of his research interests. In my second year at Alberta, then, I was acting chairman of a department which was barely getting underway.

During my year we spent a great deal of time discussing a graduate program. Everyone in the department seemed eager to offer graduate degrees. Finally, we cobbled together a program which I submitted to the graduate school and had accepted. Happily, we were a small department and I was not overburdened with other obligations.

In Amherst, years before, I had attended Friends' meetings, after which I occasionally attended during my years of living around the Boston area. In Eugene we were regular attenders at a rather large meeting. Otherwise, where we lived there was no organized Friends' meeting. In Edmonton there was a small group of a couple of dozen people whose major influence was British rather than American. For three or four years we participated in the Edmonton meeting. I never actually joined the Society of Friends, believing, first, that I was not good enough. Friends seemed to set very high standards. Many Friends were quite politically reactionary which I found incongruous. Furthermore, as the years past I had increasing doubts about god. By the early 70's I had become an agnostic. One cannot, I thought, prove the existence of god "beyond any reasonable doubt." The arguments for god's existence seemed less tenable than those against it and I could not merely accept the belief in god by faith alone. I had grave doubts about the legitimacy of all organized religion and an increasing suspicion that the world would be better off without it.

As I have noted before, at Cornell we were active in folk and square dancing and in the Sudan did some Scottish dancing. In Edmonton there was international folk dance as well as square and Scottish dancing. I participated in the folk and Scottish dancing for a few years, but eventually became rather tired of it. Also the Scottish dancing had been taken over by a very "picky" lot who turned the affair into drudgery. Jane continued with an interest in folk dance, becoming the chief instructor of the local club. Eventually she became an instructor of dance at the University and organized an English Country Dance group.

In what follows I shall go into some detail about a major uproar which occurred in the anthropology department and lasted for almost three years. I do so because it demonstrates, particularly to those unfamiliar with the politics of universities, the kinds of machinations which do occur. It has long been my belief that a university post is by far the best kind of appointment one can have in this society, primarily because it gives one a freedom that is absent in other forms of employment. But that does not mean that universities are not centres for political finagling. Until coming to the University of Alberta I had not experienced much of it largely because I was marginal to administrative affairs. At the University of Alberta I was in the midst of it all. It is rather interesting that on first going to Egypt we encountered the political turmoil of the Suez Crisis. On going to the Sudan we faced the political turmoil of the Abboud regime. Now at Alberta we had to deal with a lesser kind of political turmoil, but one which was all the more immediate and personal.

As acting chairman I had briefly explored the possibilities of graduate student participation in the department policy making, since this idea was now being widely entertained in universities. After the graduate program was approved there were four or five graduate students, but none appeared to want to be involved in administration, so I dropped the matter. Richard Frucht, who had come to the University at the same time as I did, proved to be a source of some problems. He employed his girl friend, an undergraduate, as his teaching assistant and I, along with others, thought she was in no way qualified for such a position, one entailing correcting examinations and research papers in advanced courses with which she was unfamiliar. There were also student complaints about Frucht's teaching, especially that it was too didactic. Along with this, Frucht seemed to be attempting to push the department towards a Marxist-Leninist orientation.

When Brant returned to reassume his chairmanship we had to address the question of the direction of the department program as well as how the department was to be run. At our first staff meeting in the fall it was agreed to have a meeting with the graduate students and discuss their role in departmental affairs. When, however, the meeting was held Brant and Frucht turned it into a meeting to discuss the graduate program and particularly a program proposal submitted by Frucht. At the same time Alan and Ruth Bryan had been working on a proposal of their own and so submitted it at this time. Rather than acting as a chairman, Brant proceeded to act as a strong partisan of the Frucht program and vigorous critic of the Bryan's. Happily, he met with such opposition that a motion to adopt Frucht's program was withdrawn temporarily.

We then turned to deal with the student role in departmental affairs. Frucht argued for student election of two or three representatives to department meetings (that is, those which did not involve addressing any student's performance). As a counter proposal I favoured full participation of all students with decisions based on two thirds vote of those in attendance. The election of student delegates I saw as too readily becoming a vehicle for some ideologically committed position. Frucht's fellow travelers were actually seen as the delegates. At least it would be the ideologues who would seek such positions. In addition I disagreed with the idea of representation especially when direct participation was easily achieved. My proposal was adopted as well as another of my proposals, namely that the chairman of the meeting be someone other than the department chairman and that he be elected from the participants in the meeting. Brant had continued to act in a number of different roles which amounted to a conflict of interest: he had set the agenda for meetings, chaired the meetings, acted as secretary and as spokesman for his and Frucht's orientation.

This general meeting with graduate students continued until 1972 by which time most of the graduate students were no longer interested in participation. While it operated, I thought it worked pretty well, but clearly it demanded that students devote free time to issues often not directly related to their own pursuits. Frucht, by the way, had demanded that the meeting be called the Plenum. Perhaps he thought he was Joe Stalin.

Professor Brant continually acted throughout the following years in an arbitrary and dictatorial manner. He was constantly being manipulated by Frucht who was the power behind the throne. Whatever Frucht thought was quickly reiterated by Brant. For example, on Brant's return from his sabbatical he expressed strong reservations about any student participation in administration. Then, over night, he suddenly was a vigorous advocate of Frucht's proposal for elected delegates. I had, further, informed Brant of the problems relating to Frucht during the previous year. Yet he ignored these completely and recommended Frucht for a double increment in salary and his promotion to associate professor. Frucht had only received his PhD two years before at which time he was made an assistant professor and during this period had written two articles. For this he was to be so highly rewarded. This was in contrast to Brant's recommendations regarding two other staff members who had published more and yet Brant recommended no increment at all. Both of these individuals were critics of Brant's administration.

One of Frucht's students was allowed to enter the PhD program directly without first working for a master's degree when the department regulations stated one could do so only if the student demonstrated exceptional qualities. But this student in fact had not performed exceptionally. Indeed, he was required by his own committee (composed of Brant, Frucht and one from another department) to do extra work over the summer to overcome shortcomings revealed in his examination. In addition, department regulations stated that no one was to receive all his degrees from the University of Alberta. If he had a BA from Alberta he was not to have his PhD from the same place. This provision existed because the department was small and we believed a student should be exposed to a number of different instructors. Nevertheless, this student of Frucht's already had a BA from Alberta, but was being allowed to obtain all of his degrees there.

A major problem with Brant's administration, aside from its arbitrary aspects, was the attempt

to railroad a narrowly constructed view of anthropology and one saturated with Marxist-Leninism. I
had always believed that anthropology included four
equally legitimate divisions: social/cultural anthropology, physical anthropology, archaeology and
linguistics. And I believed that all graduate students
should have some minimal competence in each,
although they 'majored' in one. I also believed that
those in cultural anthropology should be minimally
familiar with the different cultural areas of the world,
again, even though they may specialized in one. In
the latter, I found that I was in a small minority. It
always disturbed me that at Alberta and a number
of other institutions one could concern himself with
a single cultural area, sometimes just one ethnic
community within that area, and know nothing at
all about the rest of the world, particularly when the
central characteristic of anthropology as a discipline
was the study of the whole of humanity.

The immediate issue at Alberta at this time was
the place of archaeology and physical anthropology.
Brant and Frucht attempted in various ways to
impose a program which represented one special
approach in cultural anthropology; other branches of

the field were not only of no account, they were just plain bad. Brant wrote:

> I maintain that it is anachronistic and antiquarian in the extreme to place the main thrust of a newly established program in anthropology on a natural history oriented, reconstructive treatment of cultures and populations whose descendants do not have, and have not had for several decades, any separate existence. Indigenous peoples are most meaningfully studied now, and in the future, as at best, semi-separable, culturally variant components of nation-states. These nation-states cannot be understood outside of the context of the history of the metropolitan powers, of which they were colonial outliers, and of which in numerous cases, they continue to be economic and political dependencies.

Now, while this statement is well written, it is also Marxist-Leninist rhetoric. Essentially, it advocates a narrow adherence of anthropology to a kind of applied anthropology which addresses only the relation of colonized people to the colonizers. It would abolish archaeology and physical anthropology as "anachronistic in the extreme." It therefore denies any importance to history or to the genetic character of our species. Furthermore, it would abolish ethnography as well, the writing of detailed descriptions of cultures. It, likewise, incorrectly assumes that those who challenged Brant's views were seeking to make the department one exclusively dedicated to archaeology, and a conservative archaeology at that, when such was under no circumstances true. Brant was here only inventing straw men.

Brant stated further that:

> The purpose of graduate training is not to produce walking ethnographic and/or archaeological encyclopaedias of information mainly pertinent to the history of socio-cultural units which no longer exist, nor is it to graduate junior college teachers of 'general' anthropology.

This was more rhetoric. Why shouldn't a PhD in anthropology have a considerably detailed knowledge of world cultures? What otherwise was the grounds for making any intelligent commentary on the world? And why shouldn't we provide for junior college teachers? Ours was a small unknown department and at least for the time being might do better in this area.

At last our conflict was brought to a special committee of the university chaired by the president. The committee listened to both sides. I represented the 'complainants' and now after more than two years we succeeded in ultimately resolving the problem of Brant - Frucht. The committee arranged for a co-chairmanship until Brant's five year term as chairman was ended in 1971. The other chairman was the Director of the Arctic Regional Studies program who was himself an anthropologist. Even here, however, Brant attempted various mean to obtain his own way and impose his doctrinaire view on the department. Largely, he attempted this by ignoring any consultation with the co-chairman or any department members except Frucht. Brant did not enjoy his co-chairmanship, of course, and at the end of 1970 he resigned from the university and took a position at Sir George Williams University in Montreal. This has now become Concordia University and, in any case, is not one of the better Canadian universities. Aside from taking a demotion in terms of quality of the university, Brant had to accept a position which was at the associate professor level and without tenure (He had tenure at Alberta and also had been made a full professor in 1967). Frucht continued at Alberta, but with a new chairman who was not given to his ideology, he was of less importance and influence. He died suddenly of a heart attack a few years later.

I had not understood why Brant had favored my appointment to the department in the first place, but a few years later I learned that he originally thought that I, too, was a Marxist and so would make an appropriate addition to the department. He did not realize that although I also subscribed to various radical ideas and even sympathized to a limited extent with his view of the world, I was not a Marxist and I did not like the idea of imposing an ideology on an academic discipline.

Anthony Fisher, another member of our department and one who had been a strong partisan of Brant's, was for reasons I have forgotten, made an acting chairman until we could acquire someone from outside as a regular chairman. At this time, as well, I was a candidate for promotion to full professor and was qualified to take a sabbatical leave. Both of these issues had to pass through Fisher as acting chairman. Since I had been a vigorous opponent of Brant' regime he saw his chance to punish me and recommended that I not be given the promotion. To this I wrote a long statement in favour of the promotion and was ready to submit it to the faculty committee which decided such matters (It is a committee composed of all the chairs in the several departments of the Arts faculty). In it I pointed out among other things that I had published a couple of dozen articles, as well as the book on Buurri al Lamaab and had essentially co-authored another book, "The Central Middle East", in which I wrote on the Nile Valley, a substantial part of the book. I had, I thought, given my pound of flesh. On the morning in which the committee was to hear my case, I received a call from the Dean of Arts informing me that Fisher had withdrawn his negative recommendation and I would obtain my promotion. Fisher even avoided the committee meeting, but rather had an associate present the recommendation in my case. It was all a cheap and shoddy treatment. Now I was a full professor and was granted my sabbatical. I had launched my career and my family as well.

CHAPTER V
On the Plateau

For my sabbatical I planned to travel to Europe and lands in Southwest Asia and North Africa I had not been to before. I also thought of doing a bit of ethnography in Tunisia on the island of Jerba where half the population belonged to a heretical Muslim sect which was the last remaining example of the Kharijites, an ancient Muslim movement which was puritanical and had anti-authoritarian characteristics, an unusual feature in Islam. Included in the travel plan aside from my wife and myself were our two children now eight and ten years old.

We commenced with Icelandic Airways to Keflavik, Iceland. Why would one want to go to Iceland, I have been asked. I have always been attracted to rather bleak and stark places and a country which had no military establishment was also inviting. In addition Iceland was an isolated island, a fact that appealed to my romantic notion, and a land where a kind of extensive livestock ranching was important. We rented a car to drive as much of the island as we could in a week. The vehicle was a Volkswagen with a manual transmission and I had so rarely used such a device that it was just as well that Iceland with its small population did not have much heavy traffic. This was the only car which I ever rented in which the rental agent made sure that we knew where the spare tire and tire changing tools were located. I didn't know whether this was an example of Icelandic efficiency or a forewarning about the nature of the roads. As it turned out the latter was not the case, although all the roads were dirt and gravel.

The trip from Keflavik to Reykjavik went through extensive lava fields and a treeless rolling country-side. Here we had our first encounter with the chief inhabitants of the island, the sheep. They run in open range in all the 20% of the country which has accessible vegetation. The sheep are horned, some having four horns, and the wool hangs off their backs in long strands. Further, unlike sheep in other places with which I am familiar Icelandic sheep do not graze or remain together in flocks. Rather, they are individualists, probably because they have no predators - other than man.

We stayed our first night in the City Hotel which took a bit of searching to locate. Few streets in Reykjavik had any street signs and businesses apparently did not set up any significant signs of their whereabouts. In our search we encountered a lone pedestrian walking down the street and he directed us in good Icelandic to the hotel. We, then, believing we understood, drove around the block only to encounter the same person again but no hotel. The man signaled and waved his arms in the correct direction and again we reconnoitered what we supposed was the same vicinity only to come out in the street further on and there was the same man again. On the third reconnoiter we suddenly discerned a small brass plate on the entrance to what looked like part of another apartment building - the City Hotel. Another night we spent in a school dormitory in Reykjavik. The dormitories were used in winter by students from outside the capital and, then, in summer were made available to tourists. As a town Reykjavik is a treeless and bare place - a bareness reinforced by the fact that the local architecture is constructed of cement, stucco and stone with many buildings having aluminum rooves.

We drove first to Akureyri in the north. The bridges were all one way and the railings on the sides were bent so that large trucks could pass over them.

In Mexico where there were also one way bridges each driver tried to beat the other on the opposite side in crossing the bridge. Icelanders were all much more polite. It was part of road etiquette that if one wanted to pass a car he blew his horn and the person in front was expected to pull over and stop. While the roads were all graveled, they were amply supplied with chuck holes some of which on approaching them looked like bottomless pits. They were also supposed to be two lane, but more often than not narrowed considerably. Much of rural traffic seemed to be by Land Rover. These were also used in farm work, especially in hauling hay. Since it is such a damp climate, hay has to be turned often frequently and it would appear that a hay tedder is one of the most commonly used machines. The ubiquitous sheep were scattered over the countryside in groups of two to six. Cattle, chiefly of the dairy type, were pastured in fenced enclosures. We never did find out why so many cows had lost their tails. The Icelandic pony or horse is a more common sight than cattle, but they are no longer used for farm work because of the mechanization of agriculture, nor are they in demand for work in the British coal mines. Mostly they seem to stand in the fields and look out at the world, being used for a short period in the fall for the annual sheep round up or for tourists use. And they are also eaten. Farm houses were made of cement with aluminum rooves and usually attached to barns. The old style house of wooden frame covered with turf is today a rarity.

We were in the month of June so that daylight there, only a few miles from the Arctic circle, was almost twenty four hours long. At the same time it was a Saturday night when we were in Akureyri. Most of the young in the town seemed to be out doors for the entire night carousing around. On the following morning one could hear the merchants and others sweeping up all the broken glass. In Iceland at this time there were numerous restrictions on alcohol. There were no bars or any other establishments where one could drink, so people carried on their festive drinking in the alleys and streets. The sale of alcoholic beer was prohibited and the liquor stores were always on the edge of town in buildings which had no signs and had their windows painted over so one couldn't see inside.

After Akureyri we drove as far east as Lake Myvatn before turning around and returning to

Reykjavik. At this time there were no roads which completely circumnavigated the entire island.

Before arriving in Reykjavik we visited the Thingvellir region, of great historic importance as the ancient site of the Althing, the world's oldest parliament. In addition to many glaciers, Iceland has geysers and an abundance of thermal springs. The hot water is used to heat much of the city of Reykjavik as well as provide the hot water in the tap. Taking a shower meant being flooded with water which had the odour of rotten eggs. The hot water is also used to heat various greenhouses which even produce bananas.

Icelandic food was barely average. There was plenty of good fish and also mutton. We had skyr which is slightly sour cream poured into a dish. They had frankfurts on rolls served with something that resembled ketchup but was a fruit concoction.

From Iceland we traveled to Oslo in Norway where we had rooms in a university dormitory. In Norway we treated ourselves in one place to reindeer steaks. We encountered Dagfinn Sivertsen who had been a visiting professor at the University of Alberta. and he invited us to a whale steak dinner which really didn't taste too much different from beef. We moved over most of the southern part of the country in another rented car, passing over high mountain pastures and around numerous fjords going through one tunnel which was several miles in length. Passing across fjords required a ferry and the Norwegians employed the most ingenious methods for packing cars into them. Roads are often hardly more than one lane affairs and they twist and turn. Getting across central Norway is a continual repetition of a basic pattern: One leaves a town or village located in a valley bottom, begins a torturous ascent often including switchbacks and hair pin turns, until one is above the valley and in a forested highland. Then one proceeds at a gradual rate to yet higher elevations to more open boulder strewn moors where cattle and sheep are summered, in a transhumant fashion. Even at these lonely heights there were in summer the inevitable tourist hikers. From these bleak moors one can see the glaciers and permanently snow clad peaks. One then begins a descent as the road takes one again through forested areas, hair pin turns, down to another small agricultural domain and village.

Norway is truly a rugged land and many farms seem to cling onto sides of near cliffs by which if the valley wall faces the right direction they can take full advantage of the sun. Farms seemed less mechanized than in Iceland and not as prosperous. One can rent accommodations on farms and one night we spent on a farm in Ulvik, having a hearty Norwegian breakfast the next morning: skyr, corn flakes (ubiquitous in Scandinavia), various jams and cheeses, pickled fish and vegetables, boiled eggs, waffles, and fresh fruit in season. There was ample Scandinavian coffee, real coffee, not the miserable French or Italian style.

We visited an old stave church where Alan walked up the stairway to the pulpit. All of a sudden in the solemn silence of the place we heard a plink, plink, plink as the peanuts Alan had been eating rolled down the stairway. While we attempted to recover as many of the peanuts as possible it is likely that on the following Sunday the congregation would be treated to a crunching sound as the minister walked up to the pulpit.

Sweden was our next stop. One has to be on the alert to know when one passes from Norway into Sweden, since there was, at this time anyway, only a small sign indicating that you had entered Sweden. Southern Sweden appears to have some large, well kept and neat farms growing wheat and barley. The roads were certainly an improvement probably since we were now in flat country. In Upsala I locked the car with the keys inside and on a Sunday afternoon had to dig up someone who could open the car door. Swedish efficiency quickly saved the day. In Stockholm we discovered a great place for breakfast. As I recall I think it was called the Makarel. There was an enormous buffet of fruits, cereals, eggs, meats, and cheeses. One could eat there all day I suppose and we suspected that many people filled themselves up to last them until supper time.

We moved to Copenhagen from Stockholm by train. In that city we met Gordon Streib who happened to be visiting there at the time. He took us on a tour which included the Copenhagen "slums" although they appeared to us to look like middle class type apartment buildings. One cannot avoid visiting castles in Europe and this we dutifully did in Sweden and Denmark. We also noted the abundance of pornographic material available for sale in Copenhagen.

We went on through Germany and Austria. In Munich we were to change trains and had difficulty figuring out which train we were supposed to board. Practically as it was pulling out of the station we rushed on carrying our six suitcases after hauling them a quarter mile throughout the station looking for the train. Somehow Alan and Alison wound up in one car and Jane and I in another. We spent a frantic time running through the crowded train looking for them. Our search was frustrated by the fact that between our car and the one the children were in there was a baggage car through which no passengers were supposed to pass. Now all sorts of thoughts passed through my head. The kids would wonder where we were. No one understood them and they did not understand others. They might be lost to the world. Fortunately we were able to pass into the other section of the train and recover Alison and Alan. We were to spend the night on the train and I was assigned to a compartment of men, while Jane and the children were in another. Unfortunately, one of my colleagues was a loud snorer and I am a light sleeper.

This, the last lap of our railroad journey, which was to end in Ljubjana, Yugoslavia was supposedly on the famous Orient Express, but it certainly had degenerated over the years. There was no food or water available on board and the toilets were mere holes in the floor through which one could watch the passing railroad ties if one wanted to do such a thing. For several hours at the commencement of our journey the train just rolled on and on until finally there was a station stop at which one could purchase a sort of breakfast.

We spent two weeks in Yugoslavia or Yugoslobia as we not very politely dubbed it. Again we rented a car and drove over a good part of the country. At the town of Budva there was an alleged water shortage at least as far as the hotel was concerned and water was only periodically available during the day - none at all between 10 PM and 6 AM. At the same time there were water sprinklers going day and night on all the adjacent lawns. Our hotel in Ljubjana was a building of several stories and we, naturally, were on the seventh floor during a period when there were no elevators working. The main hotel in Ivanograd provided a fascinating technological display. On entering our room I moved a chair which proceeded to disintegrate in my hands; Alison entered the bathroom and the toilet chain came off her in hand. Curtains which divided the room collapsed on the floor on attempting to close them. The light switch sparkled and sputtered every time it was turned on or off and all night the toilet emitted the strangest variety of odors. When the toilet was flushed water seemed to gurgle in a drain in the middle of the floor.

Service in the restaurants was memorable. One could sit for half an hour before someone decided to wait on you and then wait a further hour before the meal appeared. We had our fill of local shish kebab and once had an unforgettable cheese omelet made from such ripe cheese it practically walked off the plate.

In Yugoslavia at this time - the reign of Marshall Tito - a tourist was expected to register his where-abouts every time he moved for the night from one place to another. We did so, however, only a couple nights, for we found that individuals rented out rooms in their homes to tourists and there was no registration and no official to take your passport. We ostensibly disappeared from the view of the authori-ties. Our first stop of this nature was at Banja Luka with an elderly couple who spoke no English, so that the old gentleman and I tried to converse as best we could in our mutually poor kitchen German. In Sara-jevo a man moved out of his apartment so we could rent it for a couple of nights. Travel in Montenegro was a highlight of the tour for its steep and rocky hills. Yugoslavia seemed to have several interesting ethnographic museums. But somehow every one we ever attempted to see was always "temporarily closed" according to a sign placed beside a listing of their visiting hours (which were also printed in the travel brochures).

In Mostar, which preserved the old Turkish flavor, we were accosted by a government tourist guide who required of us a fee to enter a mosque and then proceeded in minimal English to give us a" guided " tour. Pointing to the pulpit he told us this was where the "priest" gave his sermon and indicating the prayer niche, the indicator of the direction of prayer (mihrab), he proclaimed that this was the "altar"! Then he invited us to come down the street and be shown around an old Turkish house, after which he said that would be another charge. Despite these various, often ludicrous, encounters Yugoslavia was a most interesting experience with much to see and enjoy.

We flew from Belgrade to Istanbul where we wandered through the extensive market place and the numerous great mosques. I intended to rent a car here, but found that one could have a car and a driver for less than the price of a rented vehicle. We were given the name of Turgut Ozkan and were able to engage him for a trip throughout central and western Turkey. Turgut had worked in Germany and like so many others had after a few years returned to Turkey with savings and an automobile. He, as we soon learned, knew his country well, was familiar with good and inexpensive places to stay for a night and also was familiar with or, at least, was able to choose the best restaurants. Obviously, he was a native speaker in a land which, like the United States, was highly monolingual. All in all he was an excellent choice and it was far easier with his services rather than attempting the tour by ourselves.

Turkey has probably the best cuisine of any Middle Eastern country. The Egyptian and Sudanese fare we had once been familiar with was quite inferior to it. In Egypt the native cuisine is beans or lentils, rice, a limited amount of meat and plenty of flat bread often containing considerable amounts of corn flour. I did like mujadra which was a combination of rice, lentils, and onions. Their squabs were also good. The Sudanese diet, like Sudanese Arab music, I thought, left much to be desired. Here one was on the border between bread and porridge eaters. The bread or kisra was made from sorghum and one often started the process by using beer. At the same time one commenced beer making with bread remains. The porridge was more common in the central Sudan and it, too, was made from sorghum and was served with a hot chili sauce. In both countries certain viscous vegetables were favoured. In Sudan it was mostly okra, while in Egypt there was mulukhiyya, a spinach like plant. Sudanese ate more meat and drank more milk than Egyptians. Both Egyptians and Sudanese had dishes I found extremely difficult to take. In Egypt there was fasikh, essentially, fish that had been buried until it was rotten. In Sudan, on feast days, there was marara, raw sheep's liver. Turkish food emphasized vegetables such as peppers, egg plants, grape leaves, squash, and marrows stuffed with rice, onions and meat. There was yogurt, feta cheese, and shish kebabs and kofta. One recipe with which Jane familiarized herself was imam bayildi, a dish of egg plant with onion, tomato, garlic, parsley and basil. Imam bayildi means "the imam fainted." That is, the prayer leader was overwhelmed by the flavor of the dish. There are a number of different delicious desserts besides the well known baklava.

I have suspected that most of the Turkish cuisine was derived from the Greek since the Turks whose origin is in Central Asia as pastoral nomads were unlikely to evolve such elegant fare with so many vegetables and fruits. I have also entertained the heresy that should not be announced too loudly amongst Turks and that is that the people of Anatolia (Asiatic Turkey) are really Turkified Greeks.

Turkey is a most scenic country and it is full of archaeological sites of a variety of cultures. The Turks, I gather, have a reputation in the west as a tough and dour lot and so are not ranked very highly as a group as far as North Americans are concerned. We, however, could not take such an extreme view. Once when the car had engine trouble near a village, people came out and invited us into their home and served us coffee and snacks. I am not certain, however, that they would have done so had we not had our two young children along. In these parts, especially, the latter are always a great asset.

Dotted throughout the Turkish countryside and usually adjacent to a village are tea houses which function much like the Cairo coffee houses providing an assembly room for men to play backgammon, read newspapers and converse. While the radio was an important feature of these places in the 1970's , I would imagine that today it has been replaced by television. Women may not enter such establisments

. If a wife wants to speak to her husband in the tea house she stands outside and calls his name to come into the road and speak with her.

Near the large cities of Istanbul and Ankara there were greenhouses which had 'marshallah' written in large letters across the glass. , meaning, loosely, may god protect. This was also written on the front of big trucks and buses. In Konya we visited the famous shrine of the Mevlana Sufi order. I had been well familiar with Sufi or mystical brotherhoods in Egypt and the Sudan where they are extremely popular. In Egypt and Sudan these brotherhoods carried on a religious ritual, the zikr, aimed at inducing self hypnotic states in which it is believed the individual will experience god. There, most zikrs involved considerable bodily movement and often loud music. The Mevlana of Turkey were a bit different. They were the "whirling dervishes" who circled around in a quiet and highly dignified manner accompanied by soft and, a westerner might think, rather eerie music. Kemal Attaturk in his drive to modernize Turkey had outlawed much of Islamic practice in Turkey, including the Mevlana and other Sufi groups. The Konya centre was now more of a tourist attraction. Indeed, it was a rather unusual place since at least half of those passing through treated it as just another attraction, while others made it the object of a religious pilgrimage and offered prayers by the tomb of Rumi, the order's founder.

We traveled as far east as Sivas. To drive further east meant entering Kurdish country which Turks did not care to do for fear of the Kurds. In central Turkey the roads were unpaved and at one time we were behind a truck which engulfed us in a cloud of dust. An annoyed Turgut proceeded to pass it, laughing as he stirred up the dust in the other driver's face, to which the truck driver responded with a loud blast of his horn which rang out "La cucaracha!"

Our next destination was Tehran. We investigated the rug market where one merchant convinced us to go with him to his house where there was a much larger selection of rugs. We drove through several back streets, winding narrow ways, and were treated to tea as numerous rugs were shown to us. Actually at this time we did not have the money to purchase any rugs so in the end we thanked the man for his trouble and said we had to return to our hotel. Well, he was so incensed that he just showed us the door and left us to find our own way which we eventually succeeded in doing.

Again we were able to engage a driver and a car and see central and western Iran. Compared to Turkey Iran was in no way as scenic. The architecture of Shiraz and Isfahan were, of course, highly impressive. The food was not. It seemed that everywhere the only available dish was chello kebab, rice with broiled meat. However, this may be misleading, since Jane had a cookbook of Iranian recipes many of which we tried and were very good, including an orange chicken. Some of the sanitary conditions in roadside restaurants were quite questionable. Silverware was usually greasy and had been merely rinsed in cold water, sometimes at a local stream. The Shah, with American money, had built an extensive network of modern highways as well as a substantial military establishment, but it appeared that the rural villages had not been improved in any respects.

We were visiting Iran approximately at the time of the celebration of the 2500th anniversary of the founding of the ancient Persian Empire. From the beginning of our visit we began to hear rumors that all hotels in the country were to be commandeered by the government for its guests and that the entire city of Shiraz as well as the great antiquities of Persepolis were to be closed to all tourism. Varying dates were given for all these changes and we could obtain no consistent information from any private or government tourist organizations. No one seemed to know when the celebrations were to commence, although we were assured in Tehran that we would not be permitted to enter Persepolis. Persepolis, incidentally, is the ancient centre of the Persian Empire under Cyrus, Darius and Xerxes and was, therefore, an important site for ceremonies. We traveled on to Isfahan where we were told that one could only go to Persepolis as part of a formally organized tour group, not as individuals. But then in Shiraz we were told one could visit the place as individuals, but one had to submit his passport for inspection at the gate. Finally, after seeing the sights of Isfahan and Shiraz we drove on to Persepolis. We entered the gate, went directly to the ruins and right down a gigantic parade ground. There were no guards; no one stopped us or cared about our presence, even though at the parade grounds there were hundreds of soldiers assembled in practice for the coming great celebration.

We were able to spend several more days in Iran including trips to the western Kurdish area and north to the Caspian Sea. Alan and I decided to try the waters of the Caspian, but found there was a tremendous undertow which was rather frightening. We did not remain in the country for the 2500th anniversary. This project, by the way, was an extremely costly affair and clearly the funds would have been more appropriately used to introduce electricity, clean running water, and improved medical service to the mass of the impoverished population, but such is the nature of immense power.

One notable Iranian custom was the manner in which lower status individuals addressed those in a higher rank or the way one requested a favour from another who had a bit more power. We observed an example of this when the Tehran tourist agent prepared for us a letter to a hotel operator in Isfahan. The more inferior person approached the superior in a toadying and servile manner addressing him as 'your majesty' or 'your holiness' or the like.

In both Turkey and Iran we had occasional car problems. For both countries there is a similar pattern in dealing with breakdowns. First, when the vehicle sputters to a stop one does not attempt to move it as far off the road as possible, but may even leave it in the middle of the road. Then one begins to tinker with the engine. After a half hour of unsuccessful experimentation, the next step is to try and hail someone approaching on the road. The purpose of this, apparently, is not to get a ride to a garage to engage a mechanic, but rather to have that driver offer his diagnosis of the problem and see what he can do to fix things. Truck drivers are the best help and the most successful in this regard. When everything fails your driver may, finally, attempt to locate a garage.

We had intended to spend a longer period in Tunisia and flew there by Bulgarian Airlines which was a rather odd experience. On the plane the smoking section was on the right side and non smoking on the left so that passengers held their cigarettes in their left hand under the noses of non-smokers sitting across the aisle. The only available drink was beer. The plane, a Russian jet, was extremely noisy and rattled to such an extent that one wondered whether it was about to explode. We arrived safely in Tunis where we made arrangements to rent a small house for three months. Initially we stayed at a hotel where my pastime in the evening was to take the kids and go into the accompanying kitchenette and smack with my slipper the well endowed cockroaches that scurried about.

Our rented place was south of Tunis on the beach in the town of Nabul, which remained comfortable until December. We swam everyday until then, but now required some heat even during the day. The oil stove, however, did not work correctly because of improper fuel. This created a continuing problem for us during our stay.

At this time I had to devote a considerable amount of time to the children's school work which had been largely neglected in the past months. I had to teach arithmetic and English and I'm afraid I was not always as patient as I should have been. We sometimes went out on field trips and found many fossil shells some of which we carted back to North America. In the evenings we might march up the beach singing McNamara's Band or some other such nonsense.

We rented a car and drove around the entire country in a couple of weeks. Some of the back roads in the interior were quite incredible. On one we encountered a gaping hole - a veritable chasm - in the pavement which necessitated some time and calculation to negotiate a way around. After driving for several hours through desert and thinly inhabited countryside, the fan belt broke just as we were about to pass a gasoline station in a small town. This was a most memorable fortuitous occasion. In another community down the road the ignition key broke in half in starting the car and we were again lucky enough to locate someone who could repair it.

We visited villages where the people lived in underground dwellings and others where they lived as troglodytes in the sides of rocky hills. Such dwellings had the advantage of not heating up during the day and maintaining a more constant temperature. It is said that the underground dwellers did so in the past so that they had less chance of being observed by marauding nomads. There were beautiful beaches on the Tunisian coast, extensive olive groves, and there was the island of Jerba, the land of the ancient lotus eaters. I had thought of attempting a bit of ethnographic work among Jerba's Ibadite population, which as I have mentioned was a remnant of an old dissident Muslim movement. However, I now gave up that idea. One factor was that I have always been hesitant about field work where I am compelled to approach complete strangers and build some kind of rapport. I have never found it easy to become acquainted with people. I am just not at all extroverted. In Egypt and the Sudan I had access to individuals who provided me with an entree into the community. Here, I knew no one. Furthermore, I

found the Tunisian dialect of Arabic extremely difficult to understand and I knew not a word of Berber
which was the main language of the Jerban Ibadis.
Finally, a government bureaucrat to whom I was
directed did not seem particularly eager about my
proposal. The Tunisian government was a bit sensi-
tive about research among the Ibadi on Jerba since
they were a very conservative group and Jerba was a
major tourist centre for Europeans, including such
people as Brigit Bardot. The government was afraid
of taking any chances at stirring up any possible
conflict. Thus, we stayed on the island looking around
as tourists for a few days before returning to Nabul.

We had some contact with the enormous number
of German tourists who frequented Tunisia especially
Jerba. In general I would say that they are no better
than American tourists and possibly not as good, for
they seemed to us too often to be rude and noisy.

I used to rent a horse and ride on the beach,
but also in the countryside and in so doing became
acquainted with a few of the local farmers. The
vicinity of Nabul is a major olive growing region
with hundreds of acres of trees. Ownership is not
based on acreage, but on individual trees, so that one
person may own three or four trees in one part of the

orchard and another tree or two some place else while around him other trees are owned by a number of other people. A good part of this situation has arisen through the manner in which Muslim inheritance law operates since one may inherit bits of the legacy of a number of different relatives so that he owns a scattering of trees.

The Tunisians often rode donkeys so that when I encountered a donkey rider, the donkey would invariably begin his noisy greeting to my horse. One time I rode the horse back to our little house and put Alison in the saddle while Alan was supposed to lead the horse. Unfortunately, they moved in the direction of the horse's home. The horse first commenced a fast walk, then a trot by which time Alan had let go of the reins. With Alison on board and with no control, the horse cantered off. Alison fell off, happily, in the soft beach sands. She has never ridden a horse since then.

In February we decided to go to Morocco. Our plane stopped on route in Algiers where we waited a while in the airport. By a newsstand there was a revolving postcard holder which Alan proceeded to turn. As he did so, the entire contraption collapsed and postcards were strewn all over the floor. Needless to say the family moved rapidly out of the vicinity just as the shopkeeper jumped over the counter towards the mess.

In Morocco we first stayed in Casablanca where, among other things, we dined at a Vietnamese restaurant. This was our introduction to this cuisine and it has since that time always been one of my favorites. I suppose one of the advantages of colonialism and imperialism is a tendency to internationalize culture. Certainly if France had never been in Morocco and Vietnam, there would not be Vietnamese restaurants in Casablanca, but, of course, colonialism is a high price to pay for that restaurant.

Morocco is a scenic land and one where the tourist industry is quite sophisticated. We toured on well paved roads over most of the interior, the main centres of Berberdom, visiting villages, weekly markets and mountain steadfasts. In some of the suqs or markets the merchants had a little more than special interest in Alan - a fair haired, fair-skinned and rather husky ten year old. In addition to the interior mountains Morocco also has ample sandy beaches and mild ocean waters.

At last we had to work our way homeward. We first visited friends in the north of England at Leeds and then went up to Scotland going as far north as Inverness. Throughout, there were more castles, ruined and otherwise. On the Isle of Skye the road is one way and at one point we passed an overturned truck with an entire load of fish strewn all over the road. At a place where we spent the night, we had to pay periodically through a machine for heat. At another location the landlady kept opening the windows in our room despite the fact that it was still early spring. The same landlady took the bath tub plug so that we would have to have her permission in order to take a bath. We thought having dinner in a Chinese restaurant in the Scottish Highlands was also a bit odd. I have often criticized all these countries which we visited, but must also again note that despite all the idiosyncrasies we thoroughly enjoyed our visits.

Finally we visited my parents who had now settled in Falmouth, Massachusetts on Cape Cod. My mother in her childhood had spent much time with my Great Aunt Lillie who lived in Falmouth on a farm managed by her husband. She had always wanted to return there to live which they did on my father's retirement. My father now seemed to be quite critical of Alan: he didn't like his eating habits and thought he was too fat. Consequently Alan felt that his Grandfather did not like him. His relationship with his Grandfather was certainly different from mine with my Grandfather.

Eventually we were back in Edmonton where I decided that I would indulge in research on the role of the horse in human societies. This combined my interest in horses and my belief that no adequate anthropologically oriented review of the subject existed. My research was largely based on library sources where I took advantage of the, at that time, good facilities of the University of Alberta. I also relied on my observations of the horse husbandry in Iceland, Turkey, and the Middle East, as well as North America. The major thesis in this work was that "...man through the ages as he encountered and adopted the horse has experienced a special admiration for certain of its qualities. The admiration is enhanced with the advent of riding which gives added feeling of power, mobility and freedom not before or otherwise experienced. The psychological orientation so produced forms a basic theme of esteem for the horse whose expression may be diverted and modified by ecological, technological, economic or other cultural factors in either a more aristocratic or plebeian direction."

The work took more than two years to complete, but longer to get published. I sent out the manuscript to a half dozen publishers who had indicated an interest. Some of them kept it for over a year before sending me the rejection slip. Finally it was accepted by J. A. Allen, London, publishers specializing in equine studies, and they took well over a year before it was published in 1980 as "The Role of the Horse in Man's Culture" - a rather pompous title to say the least.

In my early years in Edmonton I also undertook research on the local Lebanese immigrant population and on a conservative Mennonite community. I had in Oregon done some work with conservative Mennonite and Molokan groups focusing on the restrictions they placed upon themselves as boundary maintaining devices. In Alberta I went to the Holdeman Mennonite community in Linden, near Calgary. I thought this group had some theoretical significance since as a Protestant body they did not follow Max Weber's conception of the Protestant ethic. Among other things they rejected both the taking and receiving of interest. They did, however, engage in business activities as petty capitalists. As I read somewhere else, I began to suspect that maybe Weber's Protestant ethic was not so much a feature of Protestantism as it was a characteristic of certain marginal religious groups which embraced this work ethic as a way of achieving success in a world dominated by a much larger and more powerful group. The Jains , Ismailis and Parsis in India, as well as the Jews and the Friends were tiny minorities whose members were noted for their achievement in the business and professional world.

The work among the Lebanese immigrants was concentrated on the Lac La Biche area. Here, Muslim Arab immigrants were largely engaged in keeping mink for their furs. Even the imam of the mosque was a mink rancher. A few years following my visits to Lac La Biche the mink business collapsed and most of the mink keepers were looking for new sources of income. Many of the Lebanese-Canadians moved to Edmonton, but before doing so Lac La Biche had the highest percentage of Muslims of any community in Canada at almost twenty per cent.

The Sabbatical had greatly enriched and enhanced several of the courses which I taught especially the course on the people of North Africa and Southwest

Asia, another on the nature of culture, and one on peasant societies. I began to teach a new course on political anthropology in which I stressed various peoples who had no government. Another course I liked to offer was on pastoral societies. It allowed me to deal with peoples in Central Asia which was of growing interest to me. However, it seemed that few students were interested in this topic so the course was dropped. There were also seminars.

In my first years at Alberta I supervised a couple of masters' theses and one PhD. When I went off on the Sabbatical I was in the process of supervising two other PhD theses. One of my colleagues took over the supervision, rushing the candidates through to completion before I returned, thus essentially stealing them so that he might have the credit for the work involved. One of the theses was on rural Egypt and this professor knew no more about Egypt than where it was located on a map. Further, he allowed the student to do the thesis without undertaking any fieldwork when one of the well established and more sensible rules of cultural anthropology was that every PhD candidate must pursue fieldwork. After this I supervised only one more PhD thesis. One of the reasons was that the chairman of the department assigned students to professors and, while there were few entering students who appeared to be interested in my areas, at the same time there were distinct cases where I was discriminated against in favour of closer friends of the chairman. A student could change his supervisor, but this was difficult since it might incur the wrath of the professor he was originally with. Once, a student whose interest was in Africa had been assigned for some unfathomable reason to a professor who knew nothing about the place. When the student learned that I was somewhat familiar with the topic and taught the only courses on Sub-Saharan Africa the department offered, he sought to change his supervisor to me, but was angrily warned by his reigning mentor that he'd better not try it.

*****

Like anyone else in the teaching business I, too, had my occasional problem with students. In an anthropology of religion course I had the students write research papers and present summaries in the class. I specifically instructed everyone that I would not accept any kind of missionizing. Papers were to be descriptive and as objective or noncommittal as possible. One student, however, insisted on ignoring my instructions, instructions which I believe were essential to any anthropological approach to the subject. When I raised the issue in the class I found that most of students were supportive of the person involved which provoked some tension between me and the students for the remainder of the course.

At another time a student was extremely annoyed because I didn't give him a good grade. He assumed that since he was in the Business School any grade he received in the lower ranking Arts Faculty should be very high. In a course on political anthropology a very self assured student never read a single assignment and proceeded to write the final examination giving only her personal opinion which actually was largely counter to anything in the field of political anthropology and, of course, was not supported by evidence. She protested her poor grade to the chairman who proceeded over my strong opposition to change it.

I once had a graduate student who wanted to do something related to art and the Middle East. I have forgotten the exact circumstances, but I recall that I did not feel very competent in the art related part of the thesis proposal and so sent it off to the head of the art department who returned a highly critical response. That I had sent the proposal to the art department and that the head had been so negative about it thoroughly enraged the student who proceeded to look for another advisor.

The biggest encounter I ever experienced with students was in a course on racism in which I roundly criticized the Israeli position and supported the Palestinian cause. This provoked student protests to the chairman of the department and on two or three occasions a group of students would attend the class and in the midst of the lecture rise in unison and leave the room. Actually the protesters were less than a dozen in number out of a class of almost one hundred. After a short while the situation quieted down and returned to normal.

Another problem began to appear before my retirement and that was a movement towards narrower focus of official interest by the department towards Canadian material. Thus, shortly after my retirement all my courses were removed and the department, particularly at the graduate level, became not an anthropology department so much as a department of Canadian Studies or even Canadian Arctic studies. Unfortunately this narrow, ethnocentric orientation seems to be common in Canadian anthropology. I once figured that if there were as many anthropologists studying modern Egypt as there are studying Inuit (Eskimos) in relation to the population that there would be about 20, 000 anthropologists investigating Egypt, probably more than all the anthropologists in the world.

In my early years at Alberta I helped organize and maintain the Alexander Ross Society which sought to give assistance to resisters to the Vietnam War who fled to Canada from the United States. I was the treasurer of the group so named because Alexander Ross was prominent in operating the underground railway into Ontario in the days of American slavery. We helped a good number of refugees who came to Edmonton. By 1973 most of the people we encountered were deserters from the US army and too many of these appeared to have deserted because they had committed criminal offenses. About this time the society disappeared. Its purpose had been accomplished.

Both Jane and I became involved in issues relating to our children's school work. We initially had placed them in an independent school where we found that they seemed to learn to read much faster and more efficiently. At the junior high school level we put them back into public school and became part of the parent-teachers association. There were what appeared at that time to be crucial issues, but which I, today, cannot recollect at all except that the major problem seemed to be personalities. There were two or three individuals who were quite autocratic. Finally, when Alan and Alison entered an academic high school there were apparently no further problems at least as far as the members of our family were concerned.

During the 1970's in summer evenings I played a great deal of badminton with Alan and Alison in our backyard. Once or twice a week we went to a lake to swim. The lakes around Edmonton were more in the nature of sloughs, being rather shallow with muddy bottoms. However, in most cases the parks department dumped sand on the edges of the lakes to attempt to cover the mud. Ordinarily it was the end of June or early July before the water was warm enough in which to swim and by September it was again too cold.

During July and August I also went berry picking. On the Indian reserve adjacent to Edmonton there were several low bush blueberry patches and I would scout them out on horseback. Strangely enough the

Indians were not much interested in them. Usually I picked 20-25 quarts. One could locate a patch and sit in the midst of it and gather a quart or two at a time. The woods in the vicinity were free of such things as poison oak, poison ivy, and crawling, biting insects. On the other hand, one had his fair share of mosquitoes. One might also pick wild raspberries and saskatoons, although we never thought the latter were ever any where near as good as blueberries. There were also high bush cranberries which seemed a useless, tasteless fruit. Some newcomers to the area would go out to pick the plentiful rose hips. Usually they only did it once since it was a nasty job having to deal with all the thorns. Coral, my horse, used to enjoy nibbling on the hips.

Even as a child I always enjoyed long walks and Edmonton afforded many good opportunities for them. While I suspect one never quite becomes accustomed to Edmonton winters, the city has innumerable places for walking and horseback riding having sixteen miles of river and creek bank trails - all flat and well maintained. In addition to being about the best form of exercise, walking is an opportunity to think and work out the problems of life. Above all one sees more readily the world around him. I am always amused and annoyed by the bicyclists who ride hard with their faces towards the ground so that they can only count the stones over which they ride and see nothing of their environment. The annoyance is provoked by their frequent rudeness towards pedestrians and horse riders. Off road vehicle riders are often even more rude. Some walkers argue that walking is by far the best way to really see things, but horseback riding is as good or better - At least it provides sometimes a different way of looking around. For example, encountering deer on horseback usually provides a better means of observation because the deer's poor eye sight means it has difficulty actually noticing that it is encountering a person. It only makes out the horse and so does not immediately scamper off.

We had in the past often gone out especially on weekends on long drives visiting various places. Now it seemed that I could generate no interest in this kind of activity any longer among family members. Indeed, I gather that for some time these ventures were not appreciated by them so that I commenced going out by myself. There eventually developed several well worn circuits that I took in the greater Edmonton area. Another activity I took up alone, primarily because others in the family were uninterested, was horseback riding. There were two or three places where they rented out rather decent horses and I used to go at least weekly for riding. I attempted to interest Alan in riding, but after a short time, he decided he had other interests. Finally, I acquired my own horse.

*****

A TRIBUTE

In the early spring of 1975 I bought Coral a three year old grade quarter horse, for $300. The odd name is from the fact that a little girl observed the horse had a small patch of coral colored skin on his nose. While he was a sorrel in his old age there was a considerable increase in white patches. He had always preferred hay, particularly alfalfa and been rather indifferent to oats, although later in life he favored a senior feed. His original owner was a layed back sort of person who did not believe in "breaking" horses, but employed his own quiet techniques instead. He had partially trained him and it was left to me to teach him to neck rein and to stand still when mounting and dismounting.

Coral had always been very placid appearing. Nevertheless, in line with typical horse psychology, he was suspicious of all things he didn't know well. The world is peopled with all sorts of dangerous or potentially threatening demons and so he readily reacted by shying. This presented problems for me when riding on the side of a road where drivers in passing cars pay little heed to you. As a quarter horse, Coral could turn on a dime which would have made him a good cutting horse. He would make such turns very quickly whenever he shied and, usually it was into the direction of the road at the presence of plastic or other odd, yet harmless objects. I was never able to convince Coral that the plastic was far less injurious to our collective health than was a passing truck or car. Another characteristic of Coral was that he liked to be up front. He sometimes became difficult to keep at a slower pace when others were ahead. Riding in a group he would not tolerate being left behind. While he was a gelding he got along best in a group of mares where he liked on occasion to herd them around. Perhaps he was what is known as high cut. That is, when castrated he was left with the seminal vesicles which continue to produce testerone.

The only time I had trouble catching Coral in

the field was when he was with a mare in heat at which time he pranced around with her. Otherwise on entering the field he would not come to me, but merely stand and look, waiting for me to come to him. On occasion I used him to help drive cattle and he really got into the act. He liked to put his nose close to the cow's tail and drive her on. Again he demonstrated his macho as a stallion would drive on his harem.

I have always thought that for a horse Coral was fairly intelligent. One day I went out to fetch him when the other horses were up on a hill by the gate. Coral was standing in the middle of a field. His ears, his whole body, were turned in the direction of some loud music being played several hundred yards away. He was greatly engrossed in the music. Another time a newborn filly happened to get into the field with several adults. Especially when they get fooling around, big horses can easily trample an infant. Coral, using recalled stallion know - how and, as if assuming the filly was his own, immediately herded all the older horses off and kept himself between them and the young one until someone came to take it back where it properly belonged. One might wonder what sociobiologists would think of such behavior. After

241

all the horse was protecting the offspring - the genes - of another horse. This was certainly not the expression of the 'selfish gene.' Was it pure altruism or pure confusion?

Coral and I had in our numerous travels been caught in some rather annoying weather. The worst is facing a hail storm when the hail stones beat unmercifully into my face. One was so bad Coral, being headed home, turned around and backed into the hail. What I feared most was being caught in a thunder storm. Surprisingly Coral did not react to thunder or lightning except one time in the midst of a wild rainstorm the lightning struck a tree not fifty yards behind us. That deafening, horrendous clap struck terror into both of us and I had a swift ride home. On another occasion we were riding through an area which had recently been flooded. The horses were slogging through water up to their hocks when it commenced to rain and thunder. It was an odd feeling to be in two feet of water and at the same time trying to take some cover under a tree in a thunder and lightning storm. I have noticed that there are various recommendations for golfers when caught in thunder storms, but not for horse riders. What can they do? At least a couple of times a year a rider is struck dead from lightening in Alberta.

One of the delights of horseback riding is that deer, as I have mentioned above, often cannot make you out, so one can stand for minutes observing them while they, pricking their big ears towards you, stare back. Sometimes they can be induced to come closer. Moose, on the other hand are a different matter. Coral viewed them with suspicion. It is a sight to see moose, which despite their funny faces look somewhat like Thoroughbred horses, effortlessly and casually hop over barbed wire fences. Coyotes were always interested in us as long as we kept our distance, although with some young coyotes I have come up to within ten feet of them. Riding in winter, when everything seems to be quite asleep, chickadees like to follow along side flying from bush to bush.

The ideal riding is a bright sunny day in September or October when the world is in a multitude of colours. Indeed, there is nothing more satisfying than riding across fallow fields or through meadows and woods on such a day. Do horses enjoy the ride as much as the rider? It seems to me that they do. Spending their days in one field does create boredom and the opportunity to go out and engage in a different activity is a change to be enjoyed. I can recall the many times we rode out to an open field and I gave Coral a nudge to which he responded with a slight squeal of pleasure, commencing a good gallop.

For a few years I found company on my rides with John Abbott, Colin Campbell and Charles Downing as most enjoyable partners. They were all engaged in the management of business enterprises. Eventually John and Colin moved to Toronto and Charlie died after years of heart problems. My riding years, while not yet over, were primarily in Alberta and have been the peak of my life's enjoyment. Much of this was in the Stony Plain Indian Reserve adjacent to Edmonton. I have always been grateful for having free access to this attractive location.

For the last few years, living in the Okanagan area of British Columbia, Kalamalka Park and the Coldstream Ranch provided the most scenic of rides, but as Coral advanced in years he no longer tolerated the struggles up hills. We, then, limited ourselves to the flat ground. As I write, Coral approaches thirty two years old and I certainly owe him much. He has always been a most willing partner, although I have not always been very patient with him which is a chronic problem with me. I think that Coral has carried me several thousand hours and about 25, 000 miles. We have seen fields of blooming prairie crocuses in April, stretches of purple fireweed in August, the gold of poplars and aspens in fall, and the grey, bleak and quiet cold of winter.

A problem that I have never fully resolved has been the reconciliation of the long hours I have spent enjoying horseback riding with my opposition to the use of violence and to forms of domination. Dealing with any domesticated animal entails the use of reward and punishment and the maintenance of dominance. This is clearly so with riding and driving horses. The use of the bit, hacamore, reins and spurs mean the infliction of restraint and sometimes pain and the domination of the animal. Even the fact that one sits on the back of a horse means ruling over him. The main reason an untrained horse bucks when mounted or even when a saddle is applied is that such acts are identified by the unknowing horse with being jumped on by a predator. The rider essentially is a predator of a different sort aiming not to eat the animal, but to exploit it. On the other hand, perhaps exploit may be too sharp a word.

I have rationalized my relationship to the horse as

ON THE PLATEAU

follows: I provide the horse with decent food, water, including water that is heated in winter, protection from the wind and storms, give him inoculations against disease and worm medicine and regular grooming. (It has been argued that one reason horses may have accepted domestication is that they enjoy periodic grooming). A major consequence of the proper care provided a horse has been that it can live a reasonably "happy" life to age 30-35, whereas in the wild few horses ever lived even to age 15 and that life is quite difficult.

Now one might justify his use of the horse by saying that he provides all this protection for which he expects some service in return. One might say it is a contract with the horse. Of course, it isn't a contract because the horse was never asked and even if he were he could not reply. But one can argue there is still some degree of equity involved. Indeed, with many situations it is the horse that is taking advantage of the owner. Too often today so much horse and other pet care approaches the ridiculous. These animals seem to have more attention paid them than is addressed to all the suffering poor in the world.

Many hold that the ideal relationship with the horse is to work with the animal. First, there is no need to "break" it. One may train in a compassionate fashion and the most successful trainers follow this procedure. In my own case, I must admit that I have often had some difficulty in practicing this approach. Clearly what I think rationally regarding domination conflicts too often with the emotional reaction. Secondly, it appears that horses do enjoy many activities with humans. They can enjoy a good race or a run. In the western United States and Canada draft horses are used in competitions pulling heavy loads. The driver may not whip the team, but must depend on the horses desire to pull.

No discussion of a person's relation with animals can overlook the fact that most mammals are genetically programmed to the principle of dominance. A herd of horses soon sorts out a dominance hierarchy. There is no other way the animal can think. Indeed, this was most important for domestication since the domesticate is led to believe the human is the master. Since this is the only way to deal with them there may appear to be a contradiction in opposing domination and at the same time enjoying an activity and an animal where some form of domination prevails, but when dealing with another species which instinctively follows the principle of dominance such dominance is inevitable. The animal cannot learn otherwise. While this may be so that dominance must be combined with empathy and compassion. Thus with horses as has been noted above it has been demonstrated over and over again that "training" is the most successful when one works WITH the animal in a quiet and encouraging fashion and more as a partner rather than working ON the animal in order to "break" him. This may be the resolution for the problem of contradiction.

*****

After word: Coral died on Friday, January 16, 2004 at 10:15 AM - a loss I cannot describe.

*****

While I have favored horses, Jane was fond of cats and over several decades we have had a few. One whose name was Tina acquired diabetes but, nevertheless, lived to be twenty years old. A major reason for such longevity in the face of such adversity was Jane's loving care. Another of our felines was Rufus who succumbed to liver cancer at twelve. While I have never been a cat fancier I will not soon forget observing this dying creature.

For some ten years I participated in the Alberta Wild Flower Survey. This was an attempt to record the flowering dates of several varieties of plants to better ascertain the coming of spring. I got to recognize some twenty to thirty wild flowers on my riding jaunts through the Indian Reserve. Recording such data commenced in early April, sometimes even before the snow had gone, when the prairie crocuses appeared. It concluded in August with the appearance of fireweed.

Edmonton once had an anarchist bookstore called Erehwon. I think it existed during the 1980's and I used to visit it frequently and spend evenings talking with any others who might drop in. Most of the time however there was only the store clerk to converse with. The store was based entirely upon volunteer work and therefore was only opened at limited times such as evenings and during the day on Saturday or holidays. Consequently it suffered considerably in sales prospects. Many days there were no customers at all. At last, the collective which operated the store became tired of the operation and it folded. During its existence I found it one of the few places where I could go and spend time with those who considered themselves anarchists.

I had begun to smoke in my teens, first stealing pipe and tobacco from my Grandfather. I even stole a cigar or two. Perhaps I was about twenty when I began to smoke a pipe regularly and did so for thirty years. Then, in the mid seventies, I caught a bad cold or flu so that I did not feel like smoking. When I recovered I thought that I had gone this far without smoking why should I continue. I have never understood why stopping such a habit is so extremely difficult for so many people. Perhaps pipe smoking is not as addictive as cigarettes. Happily neither Jane nor my children ever took up smoking nor were they ever interested in alcohol. I, on the other hand, have always enjoyed a drink or two of vodka or whiskey before supper.

In 1980 the Rhinoceros Party came to Alberta. It had been organized a few years before in Quebec. I became a Rhinoceros Party 'agent', a title which was acquired merely by writing to the headquarters. Some of the planks in the Rhino platform were:

1. Cut down the Rocky Mountains to allow Albertans to have a better view of Lotus Land (that is, British Columbia). Of course, in later years this would not be such a good plank given the economic and political conditions in

250

British Columbia by 2001 compared to those in Alberta.

2. Introduce left hand driving as in Britain, but do so by gradual change: first, the trucks would change lanes, then, the buses and finally the cars.(Lest one think that this is just too utterly ridiculous even for politicians and bureaucrats to dream up, I recall one time we were on Ethiopian Airlines and stopped at Addis Ababa. When we were asked to retake our seats the first class passengers were entered into the back door of the plane apparently because it was nearest to the airport and the shortest walk. They had to move forward at the same time that the second class entered the front of the plane and had to move backward, so that in the narrow aisle second class passengers were trying to pass by first class passengers coming in the opposite direction. Fat people particularly had a hard time.)

3. To enhance the tourist trade, limit future exports of water to the US to one gallon per customer and make them come here to get it.

4. A plank which I proposed demanded a resurvey of the country according to the metric system

with kilometers and hectares, replacing the old mileage and acres system. In the Prairie provinces roads had been laid out according to a mileage and acreage grid. Thus, it is necessary to fill in all these roads and construct a totally new system of roads based on a kilometric grid. This would certainly solve the unemployment problem for several years to come.

The Rhino Party adopted its name because like the politician the rhinoceros has a thick skin, is dim witted, has a short temper, and possesses little foresight. Their motto was "nous ne sommes pas des moutons" (We are not sheep). Eventually the organizers of the party became rather tired of the farce and by 1990 it ceased to exist.

I have always been a supporter of the Palestinian cause. I could never understand what right the great world powers had to force these people to give up their homeland for the benefit of another people who had been so long persecuted precisely by those great world powers. Why did the Palestinians have to pay for all the wrong-doing of Europeans regarding the Jews? And, then, when the Jews did take over and create their state of Israel they proceeded on a long program of oppression of the Palestinians, the kind of oppression which they themselves had been exposed to and so resented. Over the years the conflict between the Palestinians and Israelis has degenerated further and further into a Biblical eye for an eye and tooth for a tooth exchange, but the fact remains that the Israelis are occupiers of Palestinian traditional lands continually extending their occupation by blowing up Palestinian homes and confiscating their land to establish Israeli settlements, continually dividing the remaining Palestinian territory into small Bantustans just as the white South Africans sought to control their black African population. Of course the Israelis argue that 2000 years ago they too lived in this land and, therefore, they now deserve it, but this is a ridiculous claim. Two thousand years ago the entire ethnic map of the world was quite different from what it is today. Following the Israeli example, we should have to move all the European, African and Asiatic settlers out of North and South America, and Australia, all the Turks out of Anatolia, all the Anglo-Saxons and those of Scandinavian origin out of Great Britain. These are only a few examples from what would be a long list. And, of course, the claim that the region belongs to the Jews because god had ordained it is a myth and pure nonsense.

When I first went to the University of Alberta and discussed the Arab-Israeli conflict I found myself a part of a small minority regularly accused of antisemitism. However, over the years the atmosphere has very slowly changed. People no longer seem so ready to rush to an unqualified support of Israel. They are beginning to suspect that perhaps the Palestinians are not getting a fair deal.

In addition, I have stated opinions on the Holocaust which have not always been well received. Once when "Skeptic" magazine had an issue on the subject, I wrote a letter to the editor stating that whether or not the Nazis deliberately murdered six million Jews was essentially beside the point. What is fully known by everyone is that all these people were put in concentration camps for no other reason than that they were Jews and this fact alone was sufficient to thoroughly condemn the Nazi regime. My letter was not published, so I wonder if I was being classed as one of the unspeakable Holocaust deniers.

I have found the attempt of so many Jews to make a business out of the Holocaust to be disturbing. Finkelstein has written well on this subject. It is also disturbing that these people deny that anything comparable ever happened to anyone else. While the

254

state of Israel receives billions of dollars in reparations from Germany for the Holocaust Jewish victims no reparations are offered for the hundreds of thousands of Gypsies, or the thousands of socialists, communists, anarchists and homosexuals who also met their demise at the hands of the Nazis. Aside from the Nazi Holocaust there were similar atrocities in history: the conquest of the indigenous peoples of the Americas, Australasia and Siberia, the European slave ships are other examples. There have been Holocausts throughout history. They only reflect the evil consequences of power in the hands of humans.

Let me here emphasize that I have only the highest regard for the contributions to humanity made by Jews. No people can compete with the Jews in this respect. All human culture would be poor indeed without that contribution which has been in every field of endeavor. Jews have been among the world leaders in humanitarian efforts and in promoting social justice. It bears noting as well that Jewry is not a monolithic entity in which all Jews march lock step to the same tune. There is a variety of opinion regarding Israel among them, although most are sympathetic to the Zionist cause. It is to be regretted that they, a people who have endured more suffering than most others for being who they are, have become so entangled in the Israel debacle.

In 1980 I decided to visit Australia and New Zealand. No one else in the family cared to go along. Thus, I went alone. The flight to New Zealand was long and tiresome. I had arranged to take a bus tour from Auckland in the north down to southern tip of South Island. I recommend New Zealand. It is a beautiful country and the people are quite easy to get along with. If it were not so remote from everything I have ever known, it is one of the very few places in the world I would have no qualms about living in.

For a small place, New Zealand has a large variety of landscapes. In the north there is a rather damp climatic zone. To the south there are semi-arid grasslands and high, permanently snow covered mountains, and again in the extreme south a wet and cooler region. The latter, especially to the west of Invercargill, is one of the most overwhelming sites I have encountered, a land of great fjords. I had brought a camera with me, but soon had to put in a new film which I found impossible to do. I have always left the camera business up to Jane and now abandoned further picture taking.

In Australia I first looked around Sydney and then took a transcontinental train to Perth on the west coast. I liked train travel and this was superb, except the first night out there was a radio in the compartment playing music which could not be shut off and was considerably annoying. Tea and cookies were brought to your compartment before breakfast and in that meal there was steak and eggs. One could not merely have eggs; it had to be steak and eggs. The Nullarbor Plain (Nullarbor = no trees) was as flat as could be with only the minimal vegetation. Occasionally - perhaps every hundred miles - the train stopped at a station where there might be two or three other houses and nothing more. After hundreds of miles we arrived in Kalgoorlie where the train stopped long enough so that all us tourists could take a tour of the town. This primarily meant driving along a road lined with little houses in front of which sat available prostitutes who waved as we passed. I don't believe anyone in our train took advantage of this service.

From Perth I took a bus tour which went northwards along the coast and through the Kimberleys to Darwin. There is much sameness in Western Australia and in Australia in general. Practically all the trees seem to be varieties of eucalyptus and there is much spinifex, a short and sharp desert plant that make walking somewhat of a trial. The Kimberleys were an interesting scenic area. Throughout, we occasionally saw kangaroos and emus. Much of northern Australia is cattle country, although the cattle are only rarely to be seen. Infrequently a "stockman" would appear from the bush. The cattle stations or ranches are enormous in size, area being figured in the square miles, and a small one would be well over a hundred square miles in size. Given the spinifex especially, the available edible vegetation is extremely sparse. We encountered this type of country well beyond Darwin into central Australia to Adelaide.

It is interesting that such a vast and primarily pastoral land as Australia is actually inhabited by an extremely urban population that, at least as far as I could see, did not like and indeed, seemed afraid of the "outback." Except for a British passenger and me all my fellow travelers on the bus were Australians who preferred to see their country this way rather than taking their own car. How many Americans or Canadians choose to see their country on a tour bus?

Jane Barclay

1956   *ca 2000*

Harold Glenburn, Mabel, Alison,
Harold and Alan Barclay
ca 1980

From Darwin I rode the "Ghan" railroad to Adelaide. It is called the "Ghan" because the route taken followed one used by Afghan camel drivers who were here in the nineteenth century. The railroad is constructed over such unstable ground for most of the way to Adelaide that the train must go extremely slowly.

Adelaide is an attractive city where on visiting a local park I was presented with a koala bear to hold. While they might appear cuddly and cute I doubt they would make great pets. They are rather dim witted and their breath has the strong odour of cough drops from the eucalyptus leaves they subsist upon. In holding a koala one has to be careful not to frighten them, since they will immediately dig in their extremely sharp claws causing their holder some pain.

I should note that Australia possesses some of the most magnificent beaches in the world. Sandy beaches go on for hundreds of miles and the water is warm, but most unfortunately the waters are dangerous. Not only are there an abundance of sharks, but even more important are the sea wasps, a species of jelly fish with stinging tentacles which can paralyze a person. In Australia I swam in motel pools.

Incidentally, as a people Australians are much like Americans: rather aggressive and ethnocentric. They are also quite racist without even realizing or recognizing it. Once, in the Kimberleys we stopped for the night and all went into the local pub which had only then been desegregated. That is, there had been one section for the Aboriginal population and another for whites. The British fellow traveler and I entered the bar and ordered drinks in what was until now the Aboriginal section. The bus driver and other passengers were deeply annoyed that we would lower ourselves to drinking in the company of Aboriginals. Finally, Australians exhibit a strong macho character: one has to be a real he-man. I much preferred the New Zealanders.

I returned to Edmonton with various artifacts including a didgeridoo, which I could never correctly learn how to play. I now began to prepare a short book on the concept of culture. It was essentially a compilation of my lectures on the subject to my introductory class and was published as "Culture: the Human Way" in 1982. In it I emphasized that culture was really ideas in people's heads that were objectified in material forms and as behaviour. It was, then, a sort of idealist orientation which expressed a neo-Kantian approach. I suggested that all cultures were comprised of several "aspects": symboling, technology, practical knowledge, beliefs, values and social structure and organization. In dealing with the dynamics of culture I criticized functionalism and, following Dahrendorf's views, suggested that one must recognize the importance of conflict in any social situation. Finally, the book criticized the several theories in anthropology which attempted to reduce culture and its mechanisms to a single factor whether it be economics, technology, race, genes or geography.

At this time the doctrine of sociobiology had become quite popular. It revived the old argument about nature versus nurture - whether inherited biological traits or acquired cultural and environmental traits were the primary explanation for human behavior. In this book I should have devoted more space to this subject since it is a vital issue. Like fads or styles it enjoys a period when the environmental cultural features are emphasized to the exclusion of the biological. Then there is a swing to the biological and the exclusion of the cultural. It is certainly true that many anthropologists have over emphasized the role of culture. Thus, Clyde Kluckhohn once asked Margaret Mead if she knew any people where the men gave birth and nursed children. But with the advent of sociobiology the pendulum has swing far in the opposite direction. Obviously I do not believe we can reduce observable human behavior to a simple biological explanation. Genetics may provide the foundation stones, the determinants of very broadly defined human characteristics. The so-called cultural universals may reflect these, although many may be determined by structural factors. That is, if, for example, one states that a cultural universal is a curb on intra-group violence, this is a feature which derives from the very nature of any social organization. Other so-called cultural universals are purely elements of any definition of culture. Language and all symbolic activity is an integral part of the definition of culture and so not an expression of an independent universal.

Even genes are not absolute determinants of characteristics, for the full phenotypic expression of many genes is dependent upon environmental factors. One of the earliest scientific evidences for this resulted from studies of human height. Immigrants to the United States who had been reared in conditions of poor nutrition bore children taller than their parents because of better food and other living conditions. In other words genes may be factors for a potential height, say of six feet, but without the appropriate environmental and cultural conditions the individual will not attain that height.

The sociobiologists may provide us with explanations of genetically determined universal human behaviors, but they do not explain the immense variety of behaviors found around the globe. It is the historically derived and learned ideas - culture - by which humans create the complex edifice which thereby allows us to understand the variety of human behavior. We require the concept of culture to explain how it is, for example, that altruism can be expressed in such a multitude of forms. And I would think that that variety is of immense importance.

After the book on culture I prepared another which I entitled "People without Government: An Anthropology of Anarchy." Here I briefly described some of the numerous different societies around the world which thrive without any state or government. It was an attempt to demonstrate that anarchy was neither chaos nor an utterly utopian dream. I pointed out that in one respect - that is, the absence of government - all humans were anarchists ten thousand years ago. Anarchy has, it seems, worked in small face to face communities, although some ethnic groups such as the Nuer or Dinka numbering hundreds of thousands have maintained anarchic type polities. Where it really requires testing is in the context of concentrated and large populations. The book did not stress the absence of anarchy in urban, modern style societies. The only example of anarchy in a modern society is during a short period in the Spanish Civil War when anarchists did organize an urban society, but, unfortunately, it suffered under war conditions and was soon ended by the combined efforts of the Communists and Fascists. I later discussed the problem of "Anarchism and Cities" in a book, "Culture and Anarchism."

I would not agree with those who say that the examples of anarchy among the small scale societies that I described in "People Without Government" have no relevance to modern industrially oriented and heavily populated communities. The very idea of the face to face interaction characteristic of small groups is directly applicable and of major importance to the functioning of large scale societies. The greatest solidarity, personal satisfaction, and dedication to the group is maintained by the direct and equal participation in decision making regarding the substantial issues confronting any community.

The Tonga of southern Africa provide yet another example. They are a matrilineal society of several hundred thousand people who were primarily gardeners. They had no centralized political system and were an anarchic society in which each individual was obligated to several different cross cutting groups, which in turn were part of a network of further obligations so that any negative action against an individual or group resulting from one set of relationships had its counter restraining effect resulting from affiliation with other groups and individuals. One's obligation to the network of groups to which he was a member acted as a device to maintain mutual aid and social control. No chiefs or police acted to impose and force "proper" behavior.

A characteristic of functioning anarchic societies is the technique for conflict resolution where the aim is primarily directed at reestablishing or maintaining group harmony rather than seeking to determine guilt and impose vengeance motivated punishment. Thus, in a conflict between groups an independent, uninvolved mediator agreed upon by both parties is chosen to consider the matter. Before proceeding, however, he will require the opposing parties to agree to his decision and he will then first attempt to bring a compromise agreement between them. Failing this he will decide the case. He is a mediator, not an arbitrator, meaning that he has no police power to enforce his decision. Agreeing to his decision is considered a moral obligation on the part of those involved. Another not dissimilar technique for dealing with conflict and wrong doing is provided by the traditional practice of some American Indian groups in their healing circles. I would highly recommend Rupert Ross, "Returning to the Teachings, Exploring Aboriginal Justice" (1996, Penguin Books) for details on this approach.

In anarchic polities as well one important feature concerning conflict is psychological. That is, in several such societies considerable emphasis is placed on anger control. It is imperative to restrain one's temper. In addition it is to be noted that the greatest number of casualties and worst kind of human conflict is warfare which is carried to its supreme climax by the state. During the twentieth century over one hundred million people lost their lives as a consequence of wars conducted by the several nation states. Stateless or governmentless societies lack the means and the motivation for conducting such mass killing.

Consensus is the primary mode for making decisions in an anarchic society. Matters of major policy require unanimity of consent or acquiescence - a sense of the meeting. Strongly dissenting factions are permitted to withdraw from the larger group. Thus, every effort is made to protect "minority" rights without jeopardizing those of the majority. Obviously, in a highly heterogeneous population such consensus would be difficult or impossible to achieve. Some have therefore suggested that consensus be reserved for matters of general principle while practical application could be dealt with by majority vote while still reserving the right of withdrawal.

As I have observed earlier in this essay in an anarchic society there is a heavy emphasis upon personal responsibility. One does not have access to the state among other things to provision the group. Today in the modern state an individual spends 30-40 % of his working hours to support, in the form of taxes, governments which proceed to spend these funds on large military establishments, top heavy bureaucracies, ludicrous frills for state administrators, bribery and corruption. In an anarchist society one would direct his energies to participating in the management of cooperative enterprises dedicated to the maintenance of the community. Productive enterprise, whether industrial or agricultural, would be administered by those responsible for it - that is, those who produce the goods. Necessary activities such as fire protection, road maintenance, water supply, medical attention or what have you would be matters of group responsibility. The several enterprises would be federated with other similar groups to provide regional oversight and service. Power would be retained at the local level and would be minimal at the upper confederated level.

In most of the simpler societies property as individually owned material things are generally limited to movable items. Communal ownership of land, the chief resource, is the ordinary practice. There are many anarchists who advocate communal ownership of all land, industrial capital, and natural resources which raises a serious question of how this is to be achieved. Perhaps anarchists are not adhering to their principles if they seek to expropriate all land, industry and resources by compelling on the threat of violence a minority to submit and surrender what they see as their wealth. At the same time it might be possible to achieve such a goal if the community at large were to ostracize those who did not conform. I should prefer to see an arrangement which allows for both individual and communal ownership but where no one exploits others. That is, individual owner-ship would therefore be limited to small businesses employing only owner operators or partners.

Above I have focused on features characteristic of existing anarchic societies which have application to the contemporary world. There are a couple of other points by way of further clarification concerning the anarchist society which should be mentioned. First, a point I have made before but deserves repetition: the ground work for any such society must be laid in the education of the young and the radical reeducation of the mass of adults all in the direction of an emphasis upon mutual aid, cooperation, personal responsibility and techniques of peace. Given the propensities and training of most people today any large scale anarchist society would never work. Particularly important is the need to develop a devotion to non-violence for there can be nothing more socially disruptive than violence and this is especially true of anarchic poli-ties. Secondly, at least a quasi-anarchist way of life can be pursued within the existing system. One may ignore and avoid government and the state as much as possible. One may join with others in cooperative societies for all sorts of purposes; mutual aid amongst neighbors can all be developed within the existing order. The Amish and Hutterites, for example, thrive through all their lives within a larger society of outsiders and maintain their own local community managed mutual aid system which has little or no dependence upon outsiders and especially the state. Perhaps, as Gustav Landauer observed, if enough people avoided the state and looked to other social relationships, the state itself might be undermined.

*****

At the university I continued with teaching although I did not have much interest in administrative issues. I once proposed to the department a course on the Ethnography and Archaeology of Antarctica. At the university all courses had to be approved by the Faculty of Arts council to avoid the likelihood of duplication of courses amongst departments. So I thought it would be interesting to see how far such an offering might go in the council. Of course, there is no Antarctic archaeology and any ethnography would be restricted to a description of the tiny scientific research stations. The department members initially thought it might be good for laughs, but then decided not to pursue the joke.

I began to go with another student to various religious meetings, the kind with which I had never before had experience. We attended various Pentecostal assemblies which were particularly interesting when the holy ghost was said to be moving. Then there was much more spontaneous participation by the congregation largely induced by the preacher's exhortation. Worshipers spoke in tongues, danced and shook. Such meetings had considerable emotional and cathartic effect. I could not become caught up in such rituals, but I was always moved by the old fashioned hymns which were sung. Some geniuses had written music which was unsurpassed in its emotional appeal. One can readily understand why such phenomena as holiness and pentecostal Christianity can attract so many. Under an effective leadership, with the appropriately evoked phrases and accompanied by the hymn music an entire congregation can be brought to a climactic emotional state. The end result of the Sufi ritual in Islam was similar. While it lacked the preacher role provoking the emotional experience, it shared in the repetition of phrases, the use of music and the congregational element in building up this experience. Sufi rituals as well induced spontaneous behaviors such a speaking in tongues and rolling around.

We also attended Spiritualist services in which the medium allegedly spoke with dead friends and relatives of the congregants. Edmonton was a gold mine of religious diversity. Dozens of different denominations were represented providing useful material for my teaching of a course on the anthropology of religion in addition to entertainment.

Although my parents had retired to Falmouth, Massachusetts, they soon began to spend winters in Florida and, then, moved there permanently. As a result, we commenced taking the Christmas holiday each year with them. My children and I enjoyed most the opportunity to swim and body surf in the ocean which most years was possible during the winter. It meant, too, the freedom from Edmonton winter. I always called winter the fascist season because one was so restricted: restricted in what one wore, in where one went and how one went. At the same time I never found Florida to be a place I would want to call home. The best living locations were on the coast which were a little cooler in summer, but the entire coast was cluttered with one condominium, hotel, motel or what have you after another. Not only that, but there were countless honky tonks, entertainment centres, golf courses, stores, and malls.

Florida provided us with a centre for visiting other parts of the American South and within a very few years we managed to cover practically the whole of the old Confederacy. Like the American Old West I found the South rather intriguing, although I did not particularly like a good part of its culture. Like the West ,which derived much of its cultural orientation from the South it, too, emphasized a macho culture with plenty of violence and added to this was the continuing saga of discrimination against black people. Even more than the West the South was characterized by red-neckism, flag waving and it was truly the land of capital punishment. But I do like their black eyed peas, grits and biscuits!

One winter holiday rather than visiting my parents in Florida we traveled to Hawai'i. First we stayed in Honolulu and drove around Oahu. I was not impressed with Waikiki beach. It was actually not very large and so overcrowded that one had to be on the beach very early in the morning if one wanted a bit of space. Like so many beaches in summer it reminded me of a colony of seals. The island of Maui, on the other hand, was quite pleasant. It had sandy beaches with plenty of room and good body surfing. However, on one occasion a wave broke directly over my head and forced my face down ward so that it was dragged along the sandy bottom. When I came up my nose was dripping with blood. Aside from all the ocean activities Maui provided numerous interesting natural phenomena.

By 1981 both our children had now been graduated from high school and commenced attendance at the University of Alberta. Alison was first interested in drama, but soon changed to classics, with which I was far more comfortable. Drama required acting and I don't believe Alison was really interested in that so much as in other features of drama, such as costumes. And I, personally, did not have a great opinion of people in the acting world. Alan started out in computer studies but found it boring and eventually ended up, for some reason, in anthropology. I find it interesting that both children chose academic disciplines so close to my own. Alan began having weekly gatherings at our house for playing dungeons and dragons and similar games. He was also beginning an intense interest in science fiction, a field for which anthropology provides numerous ideas.

I enjoyed attending agricultural fairs, although I found they were not so much what I remembered as a boy going to fairs with my grandfather. it seemed that the agricultural aspect was considerably diminished. There weren't that many displays of different fruits and vegetables anymore and the old dominance of livestock seemed to disappear. Perhaps this is connected to the general decline of agriculture. Recently I noticed that at the Calgary Stampede the primary interest of most attendants has shifted to the numerous thrill rides for hire. Most people are so highly urbanized they could hardly tell a cow from a bull and they wouldn't know how to mount a horse.

I especially liked watching the horse pulling contests. In Alberta at most fairs there were always eight or ten teams which competed with one another to see which could pull the heaviest load. Success depended upon the eagerness as well as power the horses could generate to be engaged in the competition.

In 1984 I qualified for another Sabbatical leave and I wanted to see a bit of Africa South of the Sahara. I thought also that if we ever wanted to observe any of the wild life in the natural habitat it was probably wise to do it soon since it would not be long before it became a rarity. A visit to Kenya could be made in conjunction with a return to the Sudan and Egypt where we could visit old haunts and see any old friends who might still be around.

We flew from Edmonton to Nairobi where we remained for a couple of days and where I was met on the street by a couple of con artists who allegedly wanted to talk with me about education in Canada, but were primarily interested in seeing if they could in some way have some money from me. At one point I began to wonder whether I was about to be waylaid, but for some reason they eventually let me alone after I had given them refreshment in a restaurant where they were well known by the owners.

We left Nairobi on a safari tour of the Kenyan national parks. At this time in the national parks there were really no specified roads upon which the tour guide had to travel. They could and did go off across country if they saw or thought there might be interesting animals to observe. This caused innumerable deep ruts everywhere and contributed to erosion. The guides knew that their tips would be bigger if the tourists saw more animals, especially the rarer ones. And we were shown all of the larger mammals except for rhinoceros. Once, however, we almost did see one. The guide suddenly veered off the path and rushed to a clump of bush hidden in which was a rhino. Other guides in their cars had also assembled here (They had a communication system to inform one another of favourable sightings). Some of the guides tried to race their engines in an effort to get the rhino to come out of the bush, but to no avail.

Another time our guide thought it best that we drive away as three or four apparently very annoyed elephants began to proceed at a rapid pace towards our car. We observed a lioness who was dragging a carcass of a large antelope in its jaws to its young which we found were a mile or so away. One marvels at the power of those jaws. The lions sleep most all the time, but it is the lionesses who do nearly all the work, i. e. , hunting for a meal which is then shared with the big male of the pride. There was a great variety of different species of antelopes, the most interesting were the oryxes in the drier areas. Among the numerous kinds of gazelles were the gerenuks with great long necks. Zebras comprised two different species, one in the dry regions and the other in more moist savanna zones. In the social organization of the first, the zebras had ranges rather than distinct territories and they comprised small groups or single individuals while in the second there were much larger units with an emphasis on territoriality.

We spent a fascinating night in a tree house by a pool where we could watch the animals all night long as they came to quench their thirst after dark. These included water bucks, buffalo, Thompson's gazelles, elephants and hyenas. At another location we were being shown to our quarters and were told that two nights before a lion had killed a zebra right on the porch of the place where we were to sleep. Here and a couple of other locations we were advised not to wander out after dark.

The food on this tour was another thing to be noted. Throughout we ate like royal pashas as we also had outstanding accommodations, especially given the fact that we were most often out in the bush. Kenya appeared to us to be magnificent country. It was scenic and, at an elevation of several thousand feet and at the same time being on the equator, its climate was most benign.

Many have rightly worried about the future of the wild animals in Africa and have expressed grave concern over the encroachment of human populations by both the extension of pastoral activity and agricultural cultivation. Kenya a few decades ago was self sufficient in its agricultural production. Today because of the horrendous population increase and the use of land for commercial agricultural products which are exported to the western world, there is intense pressure on the areas used by wild animals and, thus, this expansion is at the expense of the wild. If the wealthier peoples of the world wish to save the African wild, they should subsidize countries like Kenya which possesses what is a world treasure, but is itself very poor at least in part because of the economic stranglehold of the west, especially the international banks and the International Monetary Fund. At the same time much tourist activity needs to be curtailed especially where it disrupts the lives of the wild animals. Tourist guides should not be running all over the reserves chasing after every animal for tourists' satisfaction, even though we certainly did appreciate being able to see so much wild life.

Our next destination was Khartoum in the Sudan where, even at the end of February, the temperature already rose daily into the nineties Fahrenheit. The Sudan had, of course, changed since we were there more than twenty years before. Visiting the University of Khartoum we found many broken windows and other parts in a state of disrepair. Around the city pieces of plastic and plastic bags were everywhere. Before the plastic age when paper was used, paper bags could be thrown out and would disintegrate. Now with plastic they blew around forever. The Sudanese were still attuned to the old way and unfamiliar with the nature of plastic.

The city had expanded enormously. Buurri al Lamaab was no longer separated from it and was surrounded, except for the river, now primarily by rather large houses of the more well to do (who were mostly rather corrupt government bureaucrats) and these extended all the way to Gerayf, the village immediately south of Buurri. The use of river banks for agriculture had been sharply reduced and in most areas totally abandoned. We were now in the Sudan ruled by the military dictator Numayri who in an attempt to make the country more Islamic had outlawed the consumption of alcohol. We noticed, however, that in Buurri al Lamaab there were street parties where liquor was being served. Sudanese Arabs sometimes tend not to pay much attention to dictators. This was noticeable in our previous visit when despite General Abboud there was a considerable amount of open criticism of him and expressions of displeasure about his regime. When we lived in Khartoum the population was under two hundred thousand. Now it is over two million.

When we visited 'Abdallahi Muhammad Al Haj Babikr we found that he was now much more prosperous than he had been twenty two years before. His hosh (residence) now had electric lights and water was piped into the house. While once the empty lands outside the village were the toilet, now there was a toilet inside the house. When we had supper with him his wife no longer prepared kisra and vegetable and meat stew. Rather we now had bread made from wheat, shish kebab, and stuffed vegetables after the sophisticated Lebanese fashion. It should be noted, however, that 'Abdallahi himself did not think much of this fare; in this area he had conceded to the wishes of his daughters. Following a common tradition in this part of the Sudan, he had two of his daughters who were married and with children living in his household. It is very likely that the income from his sons-in-law were in good part responsible for his good fortune. 'Abd Al Rahim who was always better off than 'Abdallahi did not demonstrate much of a change in his life style.

It was indeed a pleasure to see that they were so well off. Both 'Abdallahi and 'Abd Al Rahim had done so much for me in the past and the cultural gap between us was such that I have always felt at a loss as to how properly to adequately repay them.

We moved on to Cairo where we renewed our acquaintance with the American University, now greatly enlarged in terms of number of students and size of the campus. We walked the back streets and alleys and through the Egyptian Museum. One feature was new to us and that was the weddings of wealthy Egyptians which occurred in our hotel almost nightly. Here were enormous provisions of food. The bride and groom were greeted with much fanfare and traditional Egyptian music. The guests were countless; the affair undoubtedly cost thousands and, ironically, the marriage would likely end in divorce a few years down the road.

We visited a village near the Pyramids where I had once done a bit of research. It now contained several apartment buildings and was buried in the urban expansion of Giza (the city across the Nile from Cairo). One wonders what will happen to

Egypt whose main source of income has been from its agriculture, but where the agricultural land is so limited and so precious, and a rapidly expanding population has no other place to go. The creation of the great Aswan dam has in no way resolved any of the problems of Egypt. One might say, rather, that it has exacerbated them: farmers must pay much more now for fertilizer which is completely artificial and lacking in organic matter; the Mediterranean Sea is eroding the lands of the Delta because no Nile water is entering the sea. Consequently the Mediterranean salt waters enter into and flood the entrance to the Delta. One of the last jobs I would ever want is to be saddled with solving the economic problems of Egypt. Some have suggested that an expanded tourism will alleviate the situation , but I don't see how.

Before returning home we visited London once again. I have never been much interested in seeing the usual sights of this city. When I have been in London I concentrate on The British Museum and the many bookstores. We rented a car to drive around the southwestern part of England and through Wales. Among the places of interest to me was the old home of my maternal grandfather in the small community of Horton, near Chipping Sodbury. It was still a functioning farm when we visited it, a dairy with a dozen or so cows.

From England we ventured to Ireland which I found to be as green as everyone has said. I don't know what traveling here in the summer would be like in terms of the narrow roads and excess tourist traffic, but in the Spring it was most comfortable. I have always had an ambivalence about the Irish. I recognize that for a small land it has produced far more than its share of major literary figures, but interestingly enough so many of these were productive outside of Ireland or in Ireland under British rule and not in the Ireland under the thumb of the Catholic Church. In our short visit we found the country to be a benign place.

On our way homeward we stopped off in the United States to visit relatives. Here I became terribly ill from a urinary infection, the first of several such attacks I was to have as a consequence of benign prostate enlargement. As one passes beyond middle age, I began to realize that body parts begin to break down. I had always struggled with stomach acidity, which soon was diagnosed as hiatus hernia and, occasionally in the Middle East, had a bout or two with dysentery. The odd thing with the latter was that we had spent well over a year in the Sudan in 1959-60 and never had any problems, but on our return visit I succumbed to the worst dysentery I had ever experienced, an attack which I blame on eating at the presumably prestigious Sudan Club.

Home again I returned to teaching activities, my vegetable garden and horseback riding. Our children were soon graduated from university and attempting to find themselves and their independence. It was to be some time before either really attained the latter. Alan had visions of becoming a novelist - a writer of 'speculative' fiction and in the meantime had various different types of employment. Alison eventually pursued her interest in ancient Greek culture, although a major stumbling block there was learning the language of ancient Greece.

During the Christmas holiday of 1986 we made a Caribbean cruise which visited a half dozen islands. The cruise ship is a most enjoyable form of travel in many ways: the food is excellent - there is too much of it. Further one doesn't have to think about a different place to sleep every night. However, there is not much opportunity for stretching your legs other than walking around the ship. Swimming pools are mostly hardly bigger than large bathtubs. The advantage of a Caribbean cruise is that the ship stops everyday at some island where one can get off and look around. Several days at sitting out at sea I found to be boring from our first sailing when we went to Egypt over thirty years before. With the Caribbean cruise the islands were all close enough so that there was a good deal of variety in the trip.

On cruise ships one is placed for the evening meal at a table where there are other passengers. If you are lucky they will be interesting, if not you will have duds. In the four occasions when we have been on a ship we have had both good fortune and bad in this regard. This Caribbean cruise we were teamed up with a couple of duds - two old spinsters or divorcees from Boca Raton, Florida - one couldn't tell which. From them I have rarely had to listen to such drivel. One of their main concerns was to get at the slot machines and they evidenced not the slightest interest in any of the islands we visited; they were full of "stupid black people." I got into a big argument with them when on investigating I found the extent to which the ordinary employees - the dining room waiters, cleaners and the like - were exploited. They were paid very poorly and expected to work ten to twelve hours seven days a week. Several individuals were bunked together in a room. Our spinster shipmates thought all the employees should be most grateful for being employed. On our other cruises we were more fortunate eating with good conversationalists and more understanding people.

My book, "People without Government," had received some positive reactions and is probably the only book I have written which sold more than a few thousand copies. A group of Germans now translated it and published a German edition: "Volker ohne Regierung: eine Anthropologie der Anarchie." That English may be a more efficient mode of communication is shown by the fact that the German edition took 293 pages (although a half dozen of these were illustrations) while the English version was 162 pages. About the same time a Greek group inquired about translating the book into Greek. They, however, soon encountered difficulties with the Greek government which aimed to prohibit publication of such a subversive book.

Eventually, I became of retirement age. The Canadian government had declared that mandatory retirement at age 65 was quite legitimate. The only reason possible for such a decree was to attempt to alleviate employment problems by providing for new vacancies. The university liked the idea because by requiring such retirement they were now relieved of paying high salaried senior professors and could employ newcomers at a third the amount. This certainly happened in my case where on retirement my position was abolished and by way of keeping the same number of instructors a low paid sessional lecturer was hired. I would say, however, that the university always treated me fairly. I even received recognition for such radical works as "People without Government."

The university invited all retirees to a dinner where they handed out aluminum winged objects rather than gold watches. Each recipient had to hold his gift while standing with the president and being photographed. It was interesting that the ordinarily hierarchy conscious university had invited all people retiring in this year regardless of the nature of their employment at the university. Garbage collectors, office secretaries, and university professors were all included and equally treated.

In the same year of my retirement my father died. I attended his funeral at the end of which all the family members stood at the back of the church to receive the condolences of the very considerable number of attendees. Here I was again exposed to the kind of remarks I had heard long ago: "You should hope to be half the man your father was!" or "O! I didn't know Glen had a son." It was either my half existence or non-existence.

CHAPTER VI
It Isn't Over Yet

With retirement we commenced a series of annual trips to various locations. First, we took a boat to Alaska followed by a bus journey through the state and into southern Yukon. The weather was clearly on our side for the whole trip. Mount McKinley apparently is only rarely to be observed in all its glory, but we managed to be there at a time when it was not shrouded in clouds. In the southern Yukon there was a railroad which took us through the most spectacular of scenic mountain country.

The next year we visited the four Maritime provinces. In so doing we had now visited all the Canadian provinces and territories. With the Alaska visit I had chalked up the fifty US states as well. I had done a little work on genealogy particularly of the Barclay family. In Edmonton the Latter day Saints had a facility for looking into ancestors and I took advantage of it, although it was not very productive in terms of my interests. I once enquired of a Scottish ancestral search society and they were able to push my Barclay affiliation back to James Barclay, a dyer, born in 1701 in the town of Cleish in Kinrossshire (complete with its three s's). They could not go further since by that date there were three Barclays and it was impossible to discern which would have been the correct ancestor. In Shelburne, Nova Scotia I found material directly relating to my father's family, noting that our most illustrious ancestor was Andrew Barclay(1738-1823) who had led a ship load of Loyalists during the American Revolution to the rocky shores of Shelburne where George III had given them land grants. Andrew received 300 acres, of which, it is interesting to note, not a single acre is today owned by one of his descendants, it being hinted that perhaps the land was lost due to the duplicitous behavior of certain of my relatives who controlled the land.

Andrew Barclay had had a slight reputation as a book binder and book seller on Corn Hill in Boston until the Revolution. The information concerning the Loyalists in the American Revolution was all new to me. When I was in high school we were taught about that revolution and were led to believe that all Americans supported it. No word was ever said about loyalists or the fact that an estimated one third of Americans were loyal to the British crown while another third were fence sitters taking a neutral view. This was only another indication of the nationalistic bias of American education.

Of Andrew Barclay's descendants there have been no people of note. Indeed, my mother, I always thought, had a rather low opinion of the Barclays of Shelburne County. Her view seemed to be that they were rather a shiftless lot and the only one ever to get anywhere, because he had "spunk" and "get up and go," was my father. We visited a cousin still resident of the area. In what I have come to wonder is possibly Nova Scotian hospitality we sat in the kitchen for two or three hours and were never offered so much as a glass of water. Despite my mother's unflattering opinion of the family, this was exactly the same way she and her mother as well would have behaved and I have always compared it with that of the Egyptians and Sudanese. They could be extremely poor, but any visitor would always be greeted with offers of drinks and food. Once, when I was making a census of Buurri al Lamaab, we stopped at the house of a man who had little and he asked if we would like coffee. Being unaware at the time of what was involved I agreed. This then required sending a child out to the shop to buy coffee beans and cardamon (always used in coffee in the Sudan), roasting the beans, grinding the coffee in a pestle, and boiling the grounds.

Back in Edmonton I encountered a brief bit of trouble with the income tax people. I had received a small amount in royalties in the sale of my book on the horse and each year the publisher dutifully sent some huge percentage to the Inland Revenue of Great Britain, the book having been published there. On my Canadian income tax I had declared the amount of the royalty that I obtained in the mail. Now the Canadian revenuers said I was to declare the whole amount including what had been deducted as tax to the British. This required the most convoluted and complex reworking of my taxes imaginable. All the years that the royalty had been received had to be recalculated and as a result the total income tax bill. At the same time the amounts paid to the British had to be figured in and fine had to be paid for "late payment." In addition it was necessary to apply to the British to discontinue the taxing of my royalties and this required my giving an approximate life history not once, but at different times to different individuals. Sometimes receiving a reward is just not worth the trouble, especially when it is a small amount.

On our next overseas journey we traveled to Spain, Hungary, Bulgaria and Greece. We joined a tour bus which visited central and southern Spain. In the latter there were numerous remnants of the old Islamic culture. In the cathedral in Seville one could still read sections on the walls which, in Arabic, proclaimed the unity of god and pronounced the Fatihah, the opening verses of the Qur'an. I had not realized what a hammy country Spain was. In the bars dozens of hams hung down from the ceilings. I did not find the food all that interesting and the tradition of waiting until nine or ten o'clock for supper was not at all to my stomach's liking. We visited the locations associated with Cervantes' Don Quixote, a story I have always enjoyed.

Hungary, heavily influenced by Vienna, provided innumerable rich delicacies, a steady diet of which one would suspect could have dire consequences. We moved around Hungary in a rented car and were able to cover most all the country in a week. We marveled at the names of Hungarian towns and villages, names such as Hajduszoboszlo or Kiskunfelegyhaza and Torokszentmiklos. We went as far east as Debrecen, centre of the Protestant, primarily Calvinist, part of Hungary. On the Great Hungarian Plain we watched demonstrations of traditional Hungarian horsemanship. We visited Hungary not long after the demise of the Communist regime at which time it was a most excellent place for tourists. In both Hungary and Bulgaria I understand prices began to rise rapidly soon thereafter.

For Bulgaria we had reserved space for a guided tour around the country, but we found that the Bulgarians were just entering the tourist business so that we happened to be given a van with a driver and a guide all to ourselves. Our guide was a highly educated woman of Armenian background who made our visit all the more interesting. Bulgarians had been used to paying the equivalent of one or two cents for bus rides and two or three dollars a month for rental of apartments as well as other bargain prices, but now with post-Communism the subsidies were no longer available and people were beginning to feel the pinch, some wishing for a return to the old days.

Industry in Sofia had caused such air pollution that, standing in the middle of the city, one would never know one was surrounded by mountains. The pollution was not the only legacy of the Communist era. There was always a great problem, for example, in attempting to arrange meals for us in any restaurant, because of the government method of making payments.

Throughout Sofia there were rows and rows of ugly, drab apartment houses in the "people's republic" style. East of Sofia we drove through the quite extensive region devoted to the production of roses for attar of roses. It is one of the world's major areas for growing them. However, we were there in early spring, the wrong season for their flowering.

In Greece we made reservations for another countrywide tour, but our main purpose for being here was to visit my daughter, Alison, who was spending the year at the American School in Athens absorbing both the culture of modern and ancient Greece. For anyone attracted to ancient Greece Athens is the place to be, not only because it is the cultural centre, but also because there are several institutes located there sponsored by a variety of different countries. Each institute offers free lectures throughout the year and is associated with various research activities. Together they also have extensive library resources. The devotee of classical Greece could easily spend two or three evenings a week attending lectures and other activities.

On this visit no one was permitted any longer to enter the Parthenon because of the problem of deterioration. When we had visited Greece much earlier we were able to observe this architecture more closely. Luckily, also, we were able to enter Stonehenge in England before it was closed off and Abu Simbel in Egypt before it was moved. All of the great architectural antiquities of the world are threatened by modern civilization. Their stone is attacked by acids produced by industry and automobile exhaust. The millions of tourist feet destroy still more. Even the breath of all these people eats away at the remains. Following a trip around mainland Greece we visited a nearby island and then went off to Crete for several days of more sightseeing.

A return to Edmonton meant a resumption of old habits. In 1994 my mother died at one month short of her 101st birthday. I had only arrived in Florida to visit her when the following morning I had a call from the place at which she was a resident telling me of her death. I made funeral arrangements and being unfamiliar with the area I inquired about someone to lead a funeral service. I was directed to a local Baptist minister "who was good" and made arrangements for him to conduct the ceremony. In talking with him he, as one would expect, inquired in detail about my mother's life which I provided. I also specifically requested that we not be exposed to any of 'the washing in the blood of the lamb', 'come to Jesus' baloney. I knew my mother, although a Christian of sorts, did not care for this kind of approach, nor did my sister, and I certainly didn't. The minister agreed without hesitation, but, then, after he had presented a fairly decent biography of my mother at the funeral, he had to launch into all the salvation business. Some would say it was just in his 'blood'; it was all automatic and nothing whatever could forestall the call to come to Jesus. Buyer beware of the preacher from the doxology works, as Mark Twain called it.

My father had lived to age 97 and now my mother lived to over a 100, so that one might hypothesize that I carried some fairly good genes. Supporting this was the fact that my mother's sisters lived to be 87 and 93, her father 94 and mother 87. On my father's side it was a little more questionable. As I earlier noted, of my father's nine siblings only one reached age 90.

While still living in Edmonton we made two more major trips. One was again to the Caribbean, but had the added pleasure of a trip up the Amazon to the city of Manaus.

For the most part the Amazon was so utterly wide that it was almost like a sea voyage. At least one could not have the experience of those narrow river passages with the high equatorial rain forest vegetation rising on either side that are sometimes shown on television documentaries. At one stopping point we did manage to go a short distance in a small boat down such a passage. On the shore children and others stood, some with sloths, others with parrots and tropical birds, and still others with small alligators, attempting to sell them to the tourists.

Manaus is a major interior city of Brazil. The slum dwellings along the river banks were about the worst I have ever seen. Even Cairo slums were not this bad. On visiting an old opera house in the town one of our fellow tourists inquired how the place was heated in winter when the obvious question should be 'how do you keep the place cool at any time'. We were after all close to sea level and just below the equator. Manaus is a city of over a million population, yet the only way out of it is by air or by river boat. There is no road from the coast in the east or from the west.

Another trip was to Costa Rica and Guatemala. Unfortunately I no sooner arrived in San Jose, Costa Rica than I had another prostate attack and the thought of running over the countryside seated in a car was a little daunting. When your prostate revolts it is best to be in a standing position or to lie down flat. I decided to quit the trip and return to Edmonton. Jane continued on and saw much of Costa Rica and then Guatemala, including old Mayan remains at Tikal.

Enough prostate problems inevitably leads one to the urologist and a prostoscopy where the physician sticks a wire up your penis which enables him to see what is going on. I was given no anesthetic and assured all would be painless. Well, I can say that I have never experienced such excruciating pain in my life. I practically climbed up the wall as I hollered out several profanities.

Another health issue arose that was not so much physically painful as psychically so. It became necessary to have eight or ten of my teeth crowned and at six hundred and fifty dollars a crown this was no laughing matter. Further, it was necessary only a few years later to recrown two of them. Like most others I have never found visiting the dentist very pleasant especially for removing decay and filling teeth or, worst of all, having root canal "therapy," although I will say that having crowns is tolerable. I have suspected that dentists foregather and attempt to concoct the most miserable kinds of treatment.

I have imagined the following as a transcript of a meeting of a special secret committee of dental and dental hygiene associations called the Committee for the Enhancement of Pain. Members present: Drs Paine, Cary, Blood and Root and hygienists Frost, Scales and Gums.

"First," says Dr Paine, "we need to define our mission. As I understand it it is how we may better provoke terror in our patients."

Dr Cary: "O by all means."

Dr Root: "But I think we are obligated to make things as easy for ourselves as is possible. At the same time I am sure this will enhance the patient's pain."

Miss Frost: "I would add that our aim is not only to terrify patients, but to make things thoroughly uncomfortable for them."

Miss Gums: "Right on."

Dr Paine: "Well, let's begin with suggestions for

inducing anxiety. Actually, I think that's a better way of phrasing our task."

Dr Blood: "We should get the patient properly settled in the chair. That is, his feet must be elevated above his head. That way all the saliva and nasal discharge will roll down the throat and help to gag the patient."

Dr Paine: "Also, the stomach will more easily accumulate gas and cause added discomfort. Being so inclined, I think, also adds to the anxiety. He is in a more vulnerable position and more under the dentist's control."

Dr Cary: "O by all means."

Dr Root; "Coming into the room wearing a welder's helmet should be helpful."

Dr Paine: "But they are so heavy. Let's just wear protective goggles and masks."

Dr Cary: "O by all means."

Miss Scales: "Surgical caps should also be worn."

Dr Cary: "O by all means."

Miss Gums: "Of course, we should wear surgical gowns and great big aprons."

Dr Cary: "O by all means."

Dr Root: "And rubber gloves. It is important to

enter the operating room attired in goggles, masks, and gowns and stand in front of the patient and really snap on those rubber gloves. That's always helpful."

Dr Cary: "O by all means."

Dr Blood: "We need to have extra large size hypodermic syringes with the largest needles available to jab away at the gum. These and the other instruments of torture should be displayed directly in front of the patient. Build the proper psychological atmosphere: terror."

Dr Root: "You mean we need syringes like the vets have for horses?"

Dr Paine: "Yes that's a good idea. Now, perhaps we could turn to some other ways we might increase the general discomfort of patients and increase the ease with which we can work."

Dr Cary: "O by all means."

Dr Blood: "It is very important to deny the patient any opportunity to do the natural act of spitting. This must be prevented at all costs. We need no spittoons. Just stick a tube is his mouth and if it regurgitates everything back into the patient's mouth that just makes it more interesting."

Dr Cary: "O by all means."

Dr Blood: "I also think we need to nail a piece of

slimy rubber sheet inside the mouth and the further back in the mouth, the better."

Miss Scales: "The suction tube should be freely applied and the further back in the mouth the better. Right down the throat. Spitting is as natural as urinating and, therefore, we should prevent it at every turn."

Dr Cary: "O by all means."

Dr Blood: "O my, yes, just think. We can have the rubber sheet, the suction tube, some wads of cotton, the drill and our fingers all in the guy's mouth at once."

Dr Root: "Wonderful, Blood, I think we've really got it."

Dr Paine: "I would add, however, that we should also tell the patient that they must have several root canal operations. That's a way to really worry them. Now, I think, gentlemen, that we have enough material here to make our recommendations."

Dental hygienist Elsie Gums now added that while everything which was said was good and necessary for the torture of the patient, one should not forget that in the process of cleaning teeth, one should poke as thoroughly as possible into those corners which arouse the maximum reaction. There was a common assent.

*****

Now I must admit that all the above may not be exactly fair. I have known many dentists in my life time and nearly everyone was a personable, reasonable and friendly individual. However, I remain unimpressed with much dental treatment and retain some reservations about the behavior of many dental hygienists.

*****

Freedom Press in London invited me to submit some of my writings for a collection as a book. I took a section of the book, "Culture: The Human Way," to begin with since it was no longer available in print. I also took a final chapter from another work, "People without Government "along with a few articles and reviews that related to anarchism. The final product was entitled "Culture and Anarchism."

We lived in Edmonton for over thirty years and submitted to each of its long and dreary winters. Finally, the winter of 1996-97 was the last straw. Cold, ice and snow lasted for more than five months and we decided to search for a new retirement home most likely somewhere in southern British Columbia. I had many misgivings about ever resettling in the United States, it being ever more given to militaristic and imperialistic adventurism around the world. As we traveled we did, however, venture deep into the United States and, indeed, to some of the most red necked parts of that country. It is unfortunate that the warmest and often the most pleasant climatic conditions are located where the predominant population is so full of narrow minded, ethnocentric, flag waving 'pointy heads'. Now we journeyed as far south as the border country between Arizona and Mexico and thence over into California. From southern California on up the state and through the Northwest we could stop off periodically and visit with old friends or relatives along the way. Ultimately we came to Vancouver where we visited my son, Alan, who was living there at the time. We investigated the area for possible locations in which to live. , especially the White Rock - Langley and Surrey sections, but they seemed quite crowded as well as expensive. Consequently we moved on to the Okanagan. Jane did not much like Oliver, which she considered too small, and our impression of Kelowna was negative largely because of the enormous business section through which one had to pass in going through the town. Later we learned that there are many very pleasant parts of this city and that it has an excellent parks system.

There was, finally, Vernon. We had anticipated that we might very well find nothing at all and would have to return to Edmonton to visit a second time. But it so happens that we had access to a first class real estate agent who within three or four days had taken us to two different places both of which we liked. We chose one which was somewhat higher in price than I had originally planned to pay, but I had access to a legacy from my mother so it did not mean any financial problem. At the same time we were able to sell our house in Edmonton within less than a week after it had gone on sale and at the price we were asking for it.

The new house was outside of the city of Vernon with a magnificent view of the hills and even a small bit of Lake Okanagan. Behind the house was another person's property which was a ten acre apple orchard. This meant it was in the Agricultural Land Reserve and would not be chopped up into housing lots - not for sometime at any rate. One of the main features of the house was an enormous basement with large windows looking out on the surrounding hills and a place to deposit the 3000 books of my library.

With the house came a garden plot in which I have raised over the years a considerable amount of peas, beans, tomatoes, potatoes, corn and other vegetables. The potato crop usually has provided us with enough for seven or eight months. The biggest crop has come from the strawberries - 40 quarts a year. I have also planted several blueberry bushes which yield well. However, I miss the wild low bush blueberries I used to pick in Edmonton on the Indian reserve. Those berries are more tart and have more flavour than the cultivated varieties.

We also acquired an apricot and a peach tree as well as raspberry bushes. The apricot tree has always been a big producer and has the great advantage of not requiring all kinds of sprays against a variety of pests. From it we have made an abundance of apricot jam each year. The peach tree seems to yield every other year, but when it does there are many good fruit. One year there were over a hundred pounds of peaches. But the peach tree requires a copper spray for leaf curl.

In the fall I was able to get a year supply of apples

from picking up the drops from the neighbor's orchard. This orchard did have its disadvantage from my standpoint since our vegetable and fruit garden was located adjacent to it and so was exposed to the multitude of apple sprays which were used each year. I was not that unhappy when in 2004 the orchardist cut down all his trees and planted the field in alfalfa, saying that the apples cost more than they were worth to produce.

Throughout the Okanagan there are numerous orchards, over 90% of which are apple. And this fruit, I am sure, requires more sprays over the growing season than any other. It is also compulsory to spray one's apple trees. Since the orchards are either on or close to the banks of the lakes, one can wonder how much of the poison from the sprays eventually finds its way into the lakes. Modern agriculturalists proudly proclaim the greatly increased yields and improved quality of different crops, as well as livestock, but at what expense? The amount of fossil fuels burned up for this achievement is stupendous; the types of fertilizers, herbicides, and pesticides employed pollute the earth and the water supply. Monocropping often exacerbates infestations by different pests and soil is continually being eroded. The varieties of vegetables and fruit are developed so that they can be transported long distances without bruising and have an attractive appearance. Taste and food value are factors which are ignored. Recently introduced genetically modified varieties of plants raise questions about their potential threat to health. But what is even more damning is the diffusion of genetically modified "terminator" seeds which requires the farmer to buy new seeds each season. Agriculturalists need to seriously reconsider their current methods.

Another farm problem is that concerning animal care. I know that vegetarians would have us all avoid meat and, of course, this would lead to a very rapid decline in the numbers of cattle, sheep, goats and hogs as they would never be in demand. I do sympathize with the vegetarians and believe that in some respects they have the logically most consistent view regarding animal consumption. At the same time I have never been able to divest myself of some minimal amount of meat and I would say that this is clearly true of the vast majority of the population. At least, what farmers should do is to insure some reasonably safe and comfortable life for the animals they keep. The enormous cattle feeding operations with their thousands of head crowded into pens and filled with all kinds of antibiotics are obviously aimed purely at producing beef one can cut with a fork. This is not an acceptable form of humane husbandry. Further, the waste from such operations produces all sorts of pollution. Hog and poultry production are equally at fault. Sows when about to give birth naturally seek to build nests, but in modern hog farms they are imprisoned in crates so they can barely move. This is to prevent their young from being squashed by the sow lying on them. One method of producing veal is to confine the calves so that they cannot move, apparently to make very white meat. In poultry, hog and cattle feeding operations a paramount problem seems to be crowding which induces stress and conflict. But the main problem with agriculture is that we no longer have the emphasis on the old fashioned family farm. Rather, the intent of agricultural activity is to build the biggest and most concentrated money making operation one can. It is agri-business.

Once finally settled in Vernon, I have lost my desire to travel and see other parts of the world. I still had Ethiopia and Afghanistan on my list of places to see. Of course, Afghanistan has not been an appropriate place for travel for some time, but, in addition, I suppose it is a matter of old age which inhibits one's desire to travel.

While we have lived in Vernon for seven years we have made few friends. This is in part my fault, given my reluctance to approach strangers, but it is also the fault of others as well. When we first settled here we had an open house on Boxing Day, the day after Christmas. I went around beforehand to all the neighbors and personally invited them all to drop around for drinks and refreshments. In the end, of a dozen families, only three showed up. And since then, other than saying good morning, we have had no further contact with neighbors.

One group that I have found most pleasurable is the so-called Society for Open Learning and Discussion (SOLD), a gathering of a couple of dozen primarily retired people who meet every Monday morning to discuss selected topics. Usually, one person agrees to collect data on a chosen subject and then leads the discussion on it. I have managed to keep my mind alive by leading several discussions on topics such as Arab society, Islam and terrorism, Afghanistan, the Sudan, British Columbia agriculture, and evolution. It seems to me that such a society is an excellent idea and I am surprised that it has not been more widely implemented. Of course, to make it work depends upon the right combination of qualities in the participants. Above all they must be open minded and curious about the world around them, features which, unfortunately, I do not find that common.

For three years I was the program coordinator for the local Unitarian Fellowship and in this capacity I gave several talks, sometimes on the same subject I had given at a SOLD meeting. Jane accepted the position of president of the group. The Unitarians in Vernon were few in number; we never had more than twenty people in attendance. And it was controlled by a small clique of three women who always got their way by their own aggressive postures and the reluctance of anyone else to speak up. I was unceremoniously dumped from my position because the clique did not think I was sufficiently "spiritual."

Unitarian, for several centuries, meant a belief in the indivisible unity of god and rejected the Trinity and the idea that Jesus was the divine son of god. During the twentieth century the American Christian denomination called Unitarian commenced a radical shift in outlook so that the Unitarian statement of principles today never mentions this theological position and ignores any association with Christianity. If one talks to Unitarians most are totally unfamiliar with the traditional definition of unitarian; to others the subject is irrelevant while still others reject it outright. There are a few 'old time' Unitarians tucked away in mostly Massachusetts communities who embrace the old unitarian theology. I was familiar with these when I lived there. But most so-called Unitarians and the official Unitarian association ignore their denomination's long established tradition. They have totally and radically redefined - or, better, erased - the meaning of unitarian, a meaning which was standard for 500 years. It is as if the Communist party still retained the name, but repudiated communism and the drive to abolish capitalism. Unitarians should change their name.

So what do Unitarians stand for? Often they complain about their inability to acquire and maintain members and about the difficulty in conveying to the public what Unitarianism, as it is presently constituted, is all about. This is all easily understood since in their rejection of their old tradition, in their apparent desire to be all things to all people, in their determination not to ruffle anyone's feathers, they propose a set of vacuous platitudes. We read in the official statement of principles and in numerous "covenants" and "mission statements" drawn up by Unitarian societies about a belief in peace, justice, respect, love and tolerance which, like apple pie and motherhood, are part of everyone's beliefs whether they are fundamentalist Christians, Roman Catholics, atheists of what have you.

Unitarianism in North America today is an alleged religious body which has no creed and no specific belief. At least 19th century Unitarianism in North America had some reputation as a group which stressed rational and skeptical enquiry and was wide open to scientific investigation. Today Unitarianism is a vacuum ready to be filled with all manner of cultish gimmickry and New Age fads.

One fad is 'spirituality'. To me spirituality refers to the supernatural. To Unitarians it can mean anything. As with the term unitarian so with spirituality, make of it what you want. As Humpty Dumpty said in Alice in Wonderland: "Words mean what I say they mean, no more and no less." But spirituality apparently sounds nice; it makes you feel good or, indeed, spirituality means feeling good. But as I have said it means any number of other things as well. In an article in the Unitarian journal, "The World," one writer identified it with culture. Why, if we have a perfectly good word - culture - do we need to obfuscate the situation by calling it spiritual?

There are a number of other fads embraced by Unitarians, all of which have the strong odor of alleged spirituality. Thus, they like to light candles of 'remembrance and concern' which clearly smacks of the lighting of candles before icons and saint's statues. They observe 'hug-ins' and recite such banalities as ' I love me; I love you' to one another. They have goddess worship, one of the favorites being Gaia worship, worship of the Earth goddess. There is wicca and labyrinth walking - a revival of Medieval Christian hocus-pocus. The Unitarian journal, "World," even reports the use of prayer beads in connection with this walk. There is, of all things, a Unitarian Pagan section which is an official part of the Unitarian-Universalist Association. At least one Unitarian church "has started a twice-monthly Sunday evening worship service, for the spiritually adventurous." According to the "Canadian Unitarian" these services focus on "earth-based spirituality" and include dancing, singing and sometimes drumming. Since they have abandoned ritual traditions associated with Christianity they struggle to manufacture and embrace other traditions. While they reject the Christian practices of foot washing they readily involve themselves in mutual hand washing which is allegedly derived from some unstated American Indian practice.

Unitarians have rejected their own roots and created then an empty rootless world in which they desperately struggle to embrace all manner of other people's roots. They have rejected the ritual of traditional churches, only to grasp in nostalgia for any new fad or gimmick to fill the void. But, while abandoning Christian traditional rituals, they put on the trappings of typical Christianity with their churches, ministers, worship services, hymn singing and the like, but there is no substance.

I used to believe that I could attend a Unitarian meeting, listen to something rational, and engage in interesting intellectual discussion. I have decided Unitarians are not interested in rational and skeptical investigation and analysis. I am aware that many Unitarians are not in sympathy with all this gimmickry, pop psychology, paganism and drumming. Perhaps they are practicing that Unitarian principle called tolerance, i. e. , everything goes. Just let everyone feel good.

At the time I was divesting myself of the Unitarians, an effort was being made to initiate a Humanist group in our area. We, then, commenced to hold monthly meetings at our house in which we had a few good discussions.

But Humanists have their problems, some not unlike the Unitarians. Despite their strong affirmations of atheism, they have 'chaplains' who recite invocations and benedictions and perform other rites which are ultimately derived from the Christian heritage. Too many seem to think that if we only get rid of "religion" the world would be a perfect place. To them religion is the biggest bugaboo, the most important threat to freedom, understanding, and peace. While affirming all this they see every reason to support the idea of the state and government. To them the state is some kind of benign and absolutely necessary entity which exists to protect them. Its predatory and oppressive nature, its drive to inhibit individual responsibility, its basis in violence are all totally beyond them. Perhaps in running away from the everlasting arms of the church, they seek another set of everlasting arms in the state; one religion for another.

Their opposition to religion drives Humanists into an unquestioning acceptance of Science as absolute truth. They seem to overlook the degree to which science itself can and does become captive of a given cultural milieu or worse, the interests of corporate capitalism. Scientific endeavors are dependent upon monetary grants from governments and corporations in order to undertake research. Governments and corporations, in turn, are able to command compliance by making grants to those who might further their interests. The several specific paths pursued by scientific investigation are so well trodden because they are able to attract financing from large interested sources. Other potential and even equally important if not more important paths are far less traveled or not at all because the money providers are uninterested or down right opposed. Within Canadian anthropology funding for Arctic research is clearly more readily available than that for work in, say, the Maldives or Africa. We may also question how unbiased the results of much scientific research might be when one may actually know or a have a good idea of the results desired by the money provider. Recently, there was a lowering of the recommended healthy levels of cholesterol based on a major study. But later we find that study was financed by manufacturers of drugs aimed at lowering cholesterol. With all the so-called softer sciences (especially the alleged social sciences) opportunities for corruption are rampant. I do not agree with the extreme relativism of post modernism except to support the need for a skepticism, which not only covers philosophy and religion, but science as well since science is often not so unbiased. At the same time science provides the best methodology for understanding the world that we presently have.

Like Unitarians Humanists worry about their paucity of numbers. They note that in Canada 18.5% of the population profess no religion, but Humanists number only a thousand or so. They are apparently unaware of the fact that one does not attract followers where the only tenet of the movement is a negative one: opposition to theism or as some Humanists prefer, adherence to atheism, that is, the negative notion that there is no god. This view incidentally is as much a hypothesis as the opposite, that god exists although I would maintain that the proposition that god exists is less sustainable. In any case, one can not launch a successful movement based exclusively on a negative.

In addition, Humanists might look at the successful organizations, including successful churches. I am not suggesting that they adopt any church practices. They already do that just as the Unitarians. I only would attempt to clarify why some churches are so successful and why they are not. A good case in point may be the Latter day Saints or Mormons, a denomination which has some of the most ridiculous ideas of any religious group, yet is one of the fastest growing organizations in North America. The LDS (as distinct from the LSD) provide for family gatherings of all sorts. There are study groups and discussion groups which meet regularly. Their churches are equipped with gymnasiums where regular sports activities occur. The church is a social centre, a learning centre and entertainment centre, a place for feasting all in a family atmosphere. Some denominations offer more opportunity for emotional catharsis; in others there are rituals to satisfy all the senses: incense for the olfactory sense, ornamentation, flowers, candles and vestments for the sense of sight, music - emotional music - and bells for hearing, the sacred emblems to touch and the communion wine and bread to taste.

One of the greatest celebrations in the world is Christmas. Few celebrations equal it in the configuration of elements each of which appeals to a specific sense. Consider the Christmas in the northwestern world: the prevailing colors of red and green, the sign of the cross, the odors of the Christmas tree, the taste of the turkey, the plum pudding, the sound of the Christmas music, charismatic speech, and the touch of velvets and fur. What is important about all of this, and important about most all human formalized activities, is , first, that all of these things together are emotionally evocative and, secondly, that the entire complex of events neither required nor took the effort of some central committee or creator, nor any kind of organizer. Each element is the product of one or more individuals, but all integrated in an unconscious fashion as a self organized and emergent whole.

In a similar fashion consider another far more demented example: the German Nazi movement and its spectacles. Here, too, we have the vigorous music, the color combination of red, black and white, the comradeship, the flashy uniforms and spanking medals and insignias, the immense halls and architectural wonders, the charismatic speech and symbol of the swastika. Again divergent elements are brought together as a single integrated whole not by any one creator or committee, but despite the authoritarian context, self organized into a unitary configuration and all towards the end of provoking emotion.

It would, of course, at least it seems to me, be against a Humanist's principles to manufacture such spectacles, particularly since they are intended so much to appeal to the emotion and not reason, but if you want followers for a mass social movement, reason is too dry and unmoving; you need the emotional appeal and you need more than a single negative plank such as there is no god. Thus, as one example of many, after two years the Humanist meetings at our house came to end for lack of participation. And this has been the second or third attempt over the past couple of decades to organize and preserve such meetings in Vernon.

I have never been a fan of technology. In fact I have great sympathy for Ludditism, while at the same time I recognize that modern technology offers considerable relief from depressing and oppressing labour and above all relief from disease and starvation. Finally, after everyone else had a computer, we acquired one in 2001, but I found it to be the most frustrating object I have known. It seemed so utterly capricious and, often I have come near to throwing it out the window. Nevertheless it is so convenient in so many ways.

I have mentioned the Humanists above and here would add that an e-mail site for Humanists, in which dozens of participants may discuss any topic they choose, has proven enlightening in that useful information is often provided with which I was unfamiliar. Also, it allows some insight into those who call themselves Humanists. Here, I must say that I am often amazed at the level of ignorance and the arrogance of some who knowing nothing feel free to pontificate on any subject. I never realized that, for instance, one could claim to be a Humanist and could be a "red neck" at the same time.

Sometimes in my most depressed moments, filled with frustration and anger at the outrageous nonsense which goes on in this earth, I imagine that there are four classes of people. I have alluded to this idea early in this essay and it is in part influenced by Nietzsche. Going from the largest group to the smallest, the first and the majority are the Yahoos, as Swift called them - the ignorant, the eager flag wavers and defenders of the Nation, the vigorous, yet submissive supporters of the Grand Predators(see below), believing, for example, that some cud chewing athlete deserves 20 times as much reward as a surgeon, a creative scientist or a Beethoven (of course, there are no Beethovens today since there is no music; it's all pure cacophony). They believe the Grand Predators know best and must be blindly followed like sheep to the slaughter. They believe in progress, in the more technology the better, driving to the mall in one of those extra large Silverados with the enormous "taawrs". Most commonly they attack labour unions and argue that wages are exorbitant, while they say nothing at all about the millions extorted by corporation CEOs or big sports stars.

The second group are the Aimless Wanderers, the well meaning, quiet, hard working, tolerant, who don't know where to go or where they are going. The world to them is beyond understanding whereas the Yahoos see nothing in this world which requires understanding. But, like the Yahoos, they tend to move at the behest of the Grand Predators without knowing why and not caring to ask why.

The Grand Predators are the "leaders" of the world - the heads of states and corporations, the athlete heroes - the movers and shakers who suck up power voraciously and manipulate the earth and, like enormous parasites, live off the backs of the Yahoos - who love it - and the Aimless Wanderers who are bewildered by it all.

Finally, there is a tiny class of Free men and women who rise above all the cesspools of the earth created by the Grand Predators. They know what is going on, the intelligent ones who free themselves and are the new creators.

Among the several major problems with this classification is that I find it difficult to apply. It certainly does not apply to any of the people that I know. On the other hand, in some gross fashion it often seems appropriate in referring to our species in general. John Livingston wrote the "Rogue Primate" and I am sure that no other species has been such a rogue and rampant destroyer. Humankind has grown like some cancer multiplying so rapidly that the mere fact that humans have killed hundreds of millions of their own kind amounts to little. Obviously, this roguery has been at the behest of some group identifiable as Grand Predators and usually, then, expedited particularly with the help of the Yahoos.

Death is an issue which seems never to be really

discussed in Canadian and American circles; it is a taboo subject like sex was seventy-five years ago. As I grow older, however, I tend to review the subject in my mind. Despite the fact that I become so frustrated with things as they are and complain bitterly - a true whiner - I must note that I have been extremely lucky in this life. I have succumbed to no horrendous diseases to cut short my life at thirty or forty years of age. I have avoided jail; I have never been on welfare or the bread line. I have even managed to have a few books published and get myself to believe at least that they were half way decent. I have accomplished most of the goals I have set in life, including a PhD and top of the rank of the professorial hierarchy. My acquisition of the doctoral degree was an essentially benign process under the direction of a most cordial and gracious Bob Smith.

While I have no grandchildren to perpetuate even a bit of my name, I can console myself in the knowledge that I have been able to "spread the word" to hundreds of university students. Of course, the disturbing fact about this is that within a year or two after taking a course the student will have remembered at best one per cent of the message. If I have no grandchildren, I do have two children who are productive, upright and good members of the community and a spouse who has provided a good and pleasant house and the best cuisine.

I have traveled widely to interesting places and have had much to enjoy. I wonder sometimes however how I would have coped with some major problem since I become so exasperated over little problems exploding in ranting and raving. I do not appreciate the good I have received. One thing I have learned as a result of perusing a book listing high school graduates today, decades after graduation, is that the high school stars of yesterday are clearly not the stars of later life. I note that of several hundred graduates from my class in 1941 that I am among the five with the most prestigious positions. None were the stars of 1941 and in 1941 I was at the rock bottom of the list.

Humans are apparently the only species who are aware of their very limited existence upon this earth. In an attempt to adapt to this unpleasant fact they have invented numerous theories about a possible perpetuation of life without end. These include such ideas as reincarnation, the immortality of the soul, bodily resurrection from the dead, and Nietzsche's idea of the eternal return.

There is no empirical evidence to support any of these notions. They are all illogical and unreasonable. Consider reincarnation. If I am the reincarnation of some person from the past that means that every other one of the more than six billion now living are also reincarnations from past persons. But where could these people come from? There would have to be as many people at some fixed date in the past as are now living. Indeed, there would have to be far more to account for those not yet born. It is, however, common knowledge that the population of the world has ballooned considerably even over the past century. One hundred years ago there were one and a half billion people and four hundred years ago there were an estimated five hundred million. Five thousand years ago there were probably one hundred million. So from what bodies of beings did all the present population reincarnate?

Common Christian beliefs are the resurrection of the body and the immortality of the soul. Apparently at some future date all humankind will reassemble their remains and appear as complete living bodies. Such a view is completely at odds with anything and everything we know about life on this planet. It is estimated that there have been at least 60 billion people (that is, modern Homo sapiens) over the last one hundred thousand years. If they were all resurrected this would mean standing room only on the habitable part of the earth. Of course there has never been a properly confirmed case of even one resurrection, not even Jesus. Further, if one species can resurrect why not others as well?

Another claim is that every person has an immortal soul which never dies. But what and where is this soul? Again, no one has located it and observed it. One must surmise that the notion is provoked out of a desire for the perpetuation of one's personal identity. With so many souls there would have to be some recorder who recognizes and keeps track forever of each soul. Where is the evidence for this?

Nietzsche wrote of the eternal return by which he meant that in the course of time there would occur a recombination of parts - today we would say genes - which would exactly reproduce a deceased person. While this is a probability it would be so infinitesimal as to be impossible. At present, of course, we have the possibility to clone other living beings. Some have the mistaken notion that by such a process they will reproduce themselves, but such is not the case. They may reproduce their own genetic makeup, but that entity would be able to develop its own distinct personality, its own beliefs, tastes and outlook on life. Some good solid, all American type could be cloned and the product of the cloning land in Russia and be reared as a good solid Russian. Or even if reared as that solid all American he/she would in no sense be a spitting image. Whoever has turned out exactly as his parent desired? Cloning no more provides immortality than eternal return.

Others who are uncertain about any of the above beliefs or who disbelieve them entirely may seek to preserve some degree of immortality by producing offspring or creating a work of art or a scholarly piece. Such attempts are futile. They may preserve your name for a few generations at most. For the vast majority, even in the unlikely event that one will have descendants after four or five generations, ancestors are soon forgotten. After five generations your share of a descendent's genes would be one thirty second of the total or a little more than three per cent. On this issue of descendants it is worth observing that such a high proportion of the educated produce so few offspring, while the stupid seem to be so prolific. This appears like a refutation of the evolutionary process, that the best should produce the most offspring and should survive , although as I have noted before one might expect the more educated to have greater influence on other's children.

As for works of art or scholarly productions, they are soon forgotten unless they happen to be extraordinary. Practically all books which are written are completely forgotten after five or ten years. Scholarly articles are mostly remembered for two or three years. Paintings, sculptures, music or any other art form, only on the rarest occasions, are remembered after a few years at best.

All of these beliefs and efforts are only puerile attempts to overcome and come to terms with the bare fact that life is excruciatingly short and invariably frustrating, often brutish and cruel.

Having briefly considered these human attempts to manufacture an eternal life, let us investigate some more matters which can only reinforce the idea - the fact of an exceedingly short and very finite existence on this earth for any life form including humans. Even our sun is a finite entity which is already past mid life and may have a couple of billion more years before it commences its death thralls in which case our earth will be engulfed and destroyed by an expanding sun. Every living species has as well a finite life span, more often of one to three million years, although the cockroach and a few others seem to have survived longer. Our own species, Homo sapiens, has only been around for a couple of hundred thousand years at the most. In relation to eternity and the supposed age of the present universe, our sun, our universe, all life are passing micro-moments - mere wisps in an infinitude.

Despite all, members of each species including humans strive and fight to reproduce their kind. The meaning or purpose of life for all living forms except possibly humans is exclusively one of repro-ducing and perpetuating one's genes. Why should so much energy be invested in a myriad of organisms persisting in trying to reproduce themselves for a species lifetime of a couple of million years and then to disappear forever? Ninety nine per cent of all species are now extinct and eventually all life will disappear. To what end is all this when it is all really only a passing fancy?

We have been instructed by the Hebrew-Chris-tian Bible that we are to dominate the earth, that all its resources and the variety of life forms exist for human pleasure, but what have we done with the earth in this supposed domination? In the past there have been periodic mass extinctions of species. The present generation of humans is now the cause of yet another mass extinction as we are already responsible for the demise of several thousand species. We should not, however, place all the blame on our contemporaries since earlier peoples are also to be faulted for several extinctions, e. g. , the megafauna of Australia and possibly post Pleistocene America, demonstrating the long career of Homo sapiens as destroyer. In addition to the extinction of life, modern industrial society is responsible for the widespread pollution of the air, the soil, and water and also for a process of global warming which will eventually account for only more havoc.

Despite the Biblical proclamation the purpose of humankind cannot be to dominate the earth. The Biblical proclamation is predicated on the principle of an almighty god who is the ultimate control, the omnipotent, omnipresent, the all righteous and somehow the loving creator. Obviously, the question is how can such a being be all these at once? How, especially, can there be an entity who is both an omnipotent and loving creator? What kind of love is it that allows millions of completely innocent children to suffer horrendous diseases and starvation and to die each year? The Christian god is said to have sacrificed his only begotten son by crucifixion, one of cruelest forms of execution. What sort of being of any kind - god or otherwise - would do such a thing? Certainly if there is a god he/she/it cannot be both all powerful and loving. If this god is loving, but not omnipotent, then it is not of much help. If omnipotent, but not loving then it certainly is an evil being undeserving of any respect.

I suppose the most common argument for the existence of a god is the need for a creator. It is argued that such complex entities as exist in the world would not have appeared purely by chance and must have been created by some intelligent being. Such a view, first, overlooks the long history of our universe, the billions of years in which the evolutionary process takes place and, therefore, the opportunity for chance to operate. But chance is not the only consideration. I have above mentioned self organization as a factor in the making of human cultural artifacts and suggest it would have further applications for other phenomena. Certain features in our world may so interact as to determine a specific direction or outcome. And, finally, if we posit an intelligent being as necessary to creation we must then posit yet some other intelligent force as creator of that intelligent being and so on ad infinitum. We need not carry on with this line of discussion. All the arguments for any kind of god have been adequately dispensed with many times by numerous individuals. So where are we?

Is there any purpose or meaning to human life aside from reproducing one's own genes or dominating and destroying the earth? I believe we must all recognize that we are finite inhabitants of a finite world - a world which actually is only a small space in a universe or probably more correctly a multiverse since there might be other universes aside from our own. Surely there was a universe before this one - before the so-called Big Bang. In terms of the multiverse we are not even fly specks, but we are important to ourselves and if there is any purpose or meaning it is what we ourselves give to it. We have to make the best of what we have for we do have quite a bit. The human mind has demonstrated its positive, creative and rational capacity and this is what we should concentrate upon - to create our own well being and happiness while at the same time demonstrating care and concern for the earth and its other inhabitants (Of course, the latter can be seen as a necessary part of the creation of our own well being). None of this comes through domination, through the manufacture of hierarchical structures, through aggression and hate or violence.

Now it is strongly argued that religion and a belief in prayer and higher powers is conducive to longevity and good health. It seems to me that it is not religion or prayer as such that is the important factor, but rather the fact that one can have a relaxed outlook with peace of mind and confidence. This is certainly provided by religion, but is also attainable by other means as well. Both my mother and father were religious in that they attended church and professed a belief in Christianity. Both lived very long lives, but I would attribute this not to religion, but to several other facts. First, they obviously had good genes. Secondly, they had throughout life a good diet with complete freedom from tobacco and alcohol. Thirdly, they were actively involved in doing things they liked to do throughout their entire lives. This may be the most important factor of all. They certainly did not spend their final years sitting on the couch staring at the wall, although they were not much on physical exercise. Fourth, their lives were not filled with disease, stress, crisis, and unhappiness. Supposedly 85% or so of the population have a religious affiliation. If we controlled properly for other potential factors such as those I have mentioned in connection with my parents and found that those who lived to 90 or beyond and had a devotion to supernatural belief constituted 85% of that population one might suspect some relationship, but I don't believe this has been or can be demonstrated.

Religion has a long and intimate association with human societies and its positive contribution is questionable. The greatest architecture, painting, and music have been inspired by religion as is much of the best written literature. In addition, masses of people have found solice in religion. But they have also been misled by its doctrines and practices. These doctrines and practices and religion's role in war and genocide suggest that the ultimate verdict will not be favorable to religion.

It is said that one is a radical at twenty and a rock ribbed conservative in old age. I would modify this for myself and say that from one perspective I have always been a conservative and from another I have always been a radical or rebel. This is what has made anarchism appealing for it stresses personal responsibility - a good conservative trait - as a necessary basis for the assumption of full freedom.

I know that there are self styled anarchists who may denounce the notion of personal responsibility, just as they condemn any and all "authority," but it is they who give anarchism a bad name and lend it to ridicule. No society can survive as a free society if its members do not assume personal responsibility and in our complex society do not recognize that there are specialists who are then authorities and may thus be worth listening to. The state inhibits responsibility and confounds the concept of authority. The leaders of states want ready compliance, so they induce total dependence upon the state. Leaders of states want to be accepted as "world's foremost authorities." They want submission to the authority which carries a big stick.

Another conservative idea that is close to my heart is the notion of the old fashioned face to face rural community or as Tonnies called it, Gemeinschaft. However, I would not appreciate the pressures to rigid conformity which so often characterize this type of society. Related to the ideal rural community is another conservative idea, the family. This institution has many drawbacks, but it has, I believe, served humankind for several thousands of years and, when maintained without patriarchal domination, remains a useful form of organization. But using a dichotomy such as conservative vs radical like the similar one between left and right may not be very helpful as the brief discussion above might indicate.

Lately I have become rather annoyed at the manner in which TV nature shows present the natural world as a war in which each organism is at the throat of every other one. Violence and competition are portrayed as the only characteristics of life forms. Invariably, the fact that most of the competition is carried on between species rather than within species is overlooked. No mention is made of the role of mutual aid which as Kropotkin argued in "Mutual Aid: A Factor of Evolution" is an important facet of life. Involved here are two main components: dependency and reciprocity. By definition all social animals are dependent for survival upon group life. A number of individuals acting together is a superior mechanism for dealing with danger. Grooming is enhanced when someone else is available to assist. The young especially among mammals and, particularly among humans, have a prolonged dependency. Among humans, as among many other mammalian species, the family is a kind of communist institution where each member receives according to his or her needs, and gives according to his or her ability. Among humans, and among pack animals such as wolves or lions, also, the very ancient development of meat-eating and the hunting of game is based upon a mutual dependency. Before the bow and arrow or the atlatl - fifteen or so thousand years ago - the necessary cooperation and coordination of a group of hunters was paramount above everything else and even after that time remained of no little importance. It also has been common practice for meat acquired to be shared. The mating and long-term co-residence of an adult male and female was reinforced by the male as hunter bringing meat back to a home base and sharing it with others, but especially with his mate who would be more homebound due to child rearing obligations.

Another aspect of mutual aid is reciprocity: the notion that I will help you if I can count on you to help me. Reciprocity may be either immediate or delayed. It is likely that except for humans, reciprocity among animals is of the immediate variety. Among humans, delayed reciprocity is very common. Thus, if my house burns down and my neighbor comes to help me rebuild, I would be expected to assist my neighbor to some equivalent degree later on. Since humans have greatly superior mental capacity they can remember numerous reciprocal obligations. Other animals could not keep track and would, if they practice reciprocity at all, be restricted to some form of immediate return. Hence, there is mutual grooming or exchange of different kinds of food at the same time.

The practice of mutual aid confined to some tiny local group was not viable as humans developed urban life. Thus, in early civilizations the idea of a common humanity was conceived as applicable to the co-residents of some state or empire. The ancient Hebrews of the time of Joshua and David, for example, extended the concept of humanity and moral obligation only to fellow Hebrews. As societies came to incorporate large and heterogeneous populations in often congested living conditions the applicability of a more universalized morality became quite relevant and appropriate for harmonious living.

In the first millennium BCE this universalizing and generalizing of moral obligation became major components of rising new ideologies which appeared in Palestine, Iran, India, and China. These "great religions" all taught the golden rule as appropriate for all humanity, not merely the inhabitants of a given state. As the limitation of mutual aid to a small band was not compatible with early urban society so the limitation of mutual aid to the people of a specific state was seen as incompatible with a complex world of large interacting societies.

The history of the origins of Islam is more accurately known than that of other religions, and in a way demonstrates my point. Central Arabia in the early first millennium of the present era was inhabited by various antagonistic pastoral tribes. In the fifth century the area became more involved in international trade, and small cities arose. With this came pressure to modify old tribal relationships. By the beginning of the seventh century Mohammad preached a belief in a single universal god and a brotherhood of believers. Common allegiance to Islam was to take precedence over loyalty to tribe. The notion of brother no longer had a purely kinship meaning; it and the obligations associated with being a brother - namely, reciprocity and mutual dependence - were to be expanded to include all believers, and ideally, it was thought that all humanity would eventually become believers. Of course, these ideas never worked for reasons I mention below.

Any discussion of life's processes must address

the practice of mutual aid, of cooperation, as well as that of competition. Further, an ethic of mutual aid has emerged and evolved in the course of the development of our species. It began in the small local group and was generalized first as appropriate for co-residents of a particular state; and then with the rise of the "great religions" it was universalized to apply to all humankind, such universalizing being in response to the process of urbanization, extended trade, and other characteristics of civilization.

The problem, of course, is that while the idea emerged, other practices of violence, the pursuit of power, and competition persist. Institutions such as the state and empire and a greed-driven economy arise to reinforce violence and mayhem. They induce nationalism, a throwback to an ancient tribalism. The "great religions" while sometimes teaching love and kindness as a universal, become captives of the state so that none have ever been successful in spreading the practice of a universal morality.

Morality having been grounded in reciprocity and mutual dependence, has evolved with our species. Kant invoked god to explain morality, but that is not necessary. Both the recognition of the importance of self organization and of mutual aid and cooperation are supportive of the anarchist argument.

Recently I wrote an essay, "The State," essentially a critique of the idea of the state, which combines anarchist theory and the data of anthropology. As I noted in this work the anarchist argument against the state and all hierarchical organization is strong, but the proposed alternative - how an anarchist society would function - is weak. In large part, the weakness arises because most people today are so devoted to the idea of competition and the resolution of conflict by violence, that a long period of reeducation would be a minimum prerequisite before any attempts to realise anarchist society were feasible. Further, it is most unlikely that any state is going to allow itself to be abolished. The book was published in 2003 by Freedom Press, London.

The catastrophic events of September 11, 2001 and the second United States aggression on Iraq in March, 2003 raise several worrisome issues, the most important of which is not so-called terrorism, but the nature of the United States. This issue is considerably exacerbated by the results of the 2004 presidential election which continued the outrageous Bush administration. However, the choice between Bush and Kerry was really only one between Tweedle Dee and Tweedle Dum. Kerry was only different in that he was, as of this moment, not surrounded by a gang of psychopathic advisers. Increasingly the United States seems to be dominated by a population of Yahoo predators - flag waving, super patriots totally ignorant and essentially unconcerned about the welfare of the rest of the world except as that world can be made into a facsimile of "America" or can be bent to submit to supply and buttress American world domination. It appears that we are experiencing an ever increasing "fascistization" (to coin an ugly word for an ugly process) - a frightening land filled with too many paranoid murderous lunatics who hold the power and strive to create a world empire.

Why is it that a place such as the United States can produce people like Thoreau and Emerson and many ordinary folks who are good and well meaning and at the same time rise to the status of a true Evil Empire? We have a similar question in connection with the German people who produced so many great minds and so many truly evil people. I believe the answer lies primarily in the nature of any culture. The culture shared by any people consists of several intersecting themes many of which may be contradictory or capable of distortion. Thus, in American society there is a theme of individualism which was expressed by Thoreau as personal responsibility coupled with an integration with the natural world. We also have that individualism as expressed by the gun-toters who are unconcerned about anyone except themselves. This individualism is character-ized by a selfish competition for dominance. And when this is combined with the fact that one is a resident of the richest and most powerful nation on earth, one which utilizes a highly excessive portion of the world's resources, one has a not very attractive result. Another part of the answer lies in the nature of the state: an institution which symbolizes power and predation. Those who manage a state are invigorated with the drive to power and domination and, given the opportunity, will seek to extend their control over greater and greater areas and more and more people. This is the case of the current United States.

For over thirty years I have tried to take some refuge from this Americanism by living in Canada. This provides, however, only a slight solace. Since Canada is only one tenth the size of the United States in terms of population it is, consequently, less powerful in global politics. It is sometimes said that what occurs as a new fad, cult, or style in the United States is encorporated into Canadian culture five years later. My point is that a great many Canadians in a way want to be Americans, but among other things they lack the wherewithal to be Americans. Lacking this wherewithal means that there is much envy and ambivalence towards Americans and a constant nagging and whining to be included in the exclusive club of the "Great Powers" and to be seen as an important and active player in world affairs. It also means in a positive sense that in some respects Canadian social life can be more benign and less arrogant than the American.

Canada is often touted as one of the half dozen best places in the world in which to live. That may be so, but given the status of most other places in the world this does not say a great deal. Edgar Friedenberg once wrote a book, "Deference to Authority: The Case of Canada" in which he noted the extent to which Canadians readily submit to authority. This subservience is readily observable. Where else in the world is the police force (the Royal Canadian Mounted Police) elevated to almost saintly status? If the RCMP commit wrong then you change the law so that wrong becomes right at least for the

RCMP. Throughout the country one often hears the refrain that we elected our officials and so should be obedient to them. We should abdicate our rights to our members of Parliament. The state is almost universally held to be a benevolent and necessary entity established to protect the interests of the common people.

Canada never had a social revolution and its domain has been populated by immigrants, very few of whom were seeking refuge from oppression. Nearly all the immigrants and settlers were good solid, subservient citizens. A major part of the early English speaking settlers were United Empire Loyalists moving to Canada so they could continue to be servants of the king. More than a quarter of the population is composed of descendants of seventeenth century French settlers who were good serfs and pious Roman Catholics. Later immigrants had not too dissimilar characteristics. There seems almost to have been a selective process drawing in those who would be most malleable and deferent to established authority. Only the Doukhobors represent a tiny relief from this pattern.

In addition to creating a society based on populations of subservient immigrants, Canada has other features which have encouraged deference to authority. It was a part of a colonial empire for an incredibly long time: well over three hundred years. It has maintained a highly centralized government which can best be described as a benevolent and oligarchic dictatorship. Happily, however, there has occurred in the last thirty years a change in orientation amongst the bulk of the population. Canadians today seem less subservient to authority, less so than Americans. We have numerous examples of this change, but most seem to be confined to sexual and family relations. Thus, there is acceptance of divorce, abortion, contraception, and same sex marriage and greater toleration of homosexuality. This is similar to changes that have occurred in other sections of the western world. Perhaps, also Canadians have learned to be more open and tolerant of differences in part because of the more recent and more massive influx of Asiatic peoples. While Canadians are still militaristic in their glorification of their participation in past battles of World Wars and their love of Armistice Day rituals and poppy wearing, they seem less given to the resort to violence as an alleged solution to problems. This is exemplified by the abolition of capital punishment and greater reluctance to join in on every American military escapade. As a further indication of a change in attitudes towards authority we find a greatly reduced church attendance and considerably more people who have no religious affiliation whatsoever.

I live in Canada because there are few alternatives; the dictatorship is benign; my tax money goes less for military expenses; and I presently live in the southern interior of British Columbia which is a scenic and attractive land with a reasonable climate. Finally I could not return to the land of my birth for obvious reasons.

Jane's mother died in 2001 and her sister a year later. Her father had passed away several years before. Both of her parents were kindly, generous, and, except for a few prejudices, tolerant people. Possibly her father had acquired these characteristics from his Italian upbringing. I have often thought that my own parents might have absorbed more of these features and been less obsessed with "avoiding the poor house"or as Freud might say, less anally erotic. As one might predict, it was the latter that ultimately gave my sister and me a good legacy, while Jane's parents left none.

I could never understand those people who on

retirement do not know what to do and so sit and stare at the wall. As far as I am concerned retirement has been a very busy time. There is generally too much to do in a twenty four hour day. It is especially difficult, for example, to keep up with all the important reading. I have always been a slow reader and generally cannot find adequate time in a week to finish a book. Aside from that I feel obliged to do some writing; there is the e-mail and the internet and numerous ideas to investigate. Indeed, a major problem of the modern world is that we are all being flooded with so much information and it takes so much time to sift out the truth. Until my old horse died in 2004 I rode regularly and I suspect I was about the oldest person around who continued to do so. There is still the garden to tend. In the moments in between I can reminisce on the greatest experiences of my life. I can still recover the thrill I used to have as a boy going up to my grandfather's farm. I can look back with great satisfaction at the birth of each of my two children and I can cherish those times of story telling to my son, Alan, when I used to concoct tales which combined the lives of Booboo Bear and Winnie the Pooh. I think of my reception of the Ph D degree and my first published book. There is still the joy of remembering riding out on old Coral and recalling those days in Edmonton when I rode the nearby Indian reserve with Charlie, Colin and John. Now I can attend my daughter's own reception of a Ph D and her assumption of a position as a university assistant professor. I can as well look forward to the day when my son will publish his novel of speculative fiction.

One of the things one comes to appreciate in old age is having one's children nearby. Unfortunately, thus far, this has not been my fate. Of course we chose to live in Vernon which is some distance from any main centres. Our daughter, Alison, had been appointed for a year in the Department of Classics at McMaster University in Hamilton, Ontario and now is in her second and most likely final year at the University of New Brunswick, in Fredericton. where she has been burdened with an excessive overload of work, teaching well over 150 students with no asistance in grading papers. As is typical of any beginner she devotes innumerable hours a day to class preparation. Usually when one mentions university teaching others unfamiliar with the situation invariably see it as a kind of grand holiday where you work for eight or nine hours a week. They do not realize that especially for a beginner this means forty or more hours a week on preparation alone. In addition one is expected to talk with students, make up and correct examinations and engage in meaningful research and writing. At the same time, given Alison's situation, she must also devote hours to looking for a position for next year.

Today obtaining a permanent university position is not that common. A high proportion of new PhD's are employed for a year at one university and must move on the next. This is done so that all the benefits provided permanent staff will not have to be given. They may be the lucky ones since others get no university appointment at all and work as taxi cab drivers or at other low paying jobs. This is a world totally different from that to which I was introduced in the 1950's and 60's when there was no problem obtaining a tenure track position (a position which is permanent provided you perform well in the eyes of the powers that be).

While Alison remains more than two thousand miles away, our son, Alan, lives in Seattle where he teaches writing in a community college and strives to produce that singular work of speculative fiction.

Harold, Alison and Jane Barclay
Alison receives her PhD from the
University of Toronto, 2002

Alan Barclay

Only a very few years ago I had notions of further extensive travel. Today I would just as soon see the exotic spectacles on television. As I have already noted above, it is certainly a factor of age, but also since I had the prostate attack in Costa Rica I have been more concerned about becoming ill when away from home.

Throughout my adult life I have participated in numerous demonstrations and marches in favor of peace, opposed to war and militarism and to the rulers of the world. It remains a question as to how effective such expressions are. They certainly need to be far more widely supported with really mass endorsement to make any impression. They must also be reinforced by widespread strikes and more civil disobedience. George Bush thought the demonstration of 250,000 people at the 2004 Republican convention was merely the voice of a deviant minority. He might have had different words if that demonstration had been backed up at least with numerous other demonstrations and labor strikes. This, of course, may all be pipe dreaming. That is, it is more likely that widespread demonstrations would never occur and it is more likely that they would not effect George Bush. But even if demonstrations

359

remain ineffective it is paramount that they must be carried on. It is necessary for one's self respect and moral sense, if nothing else, that one's opposition to domination and all the nonsense of the ruling elite be proclaimed.

In reviewing my various researches and writings the truly original and in any way significant contributions I have made are, like those of the vast majority of people, few and far between, but I can say that I researched and wrote the first ethnography of a Sudanese Arab community and in this ethnography I introduced ideas later to be mentioned by others, although they overlooked my initial observations. Thus, I have noted the similarities between evangelical Protestantism and Sunni Islam. I have criticized the segmentary lineage model pointing out that tribes are not always by any means composed exclusively of kinsmen, but one, as in the Sudan, finds tribes which are composed of unrelated people brought together in a locale for one reason or another. In addition, I was the first to gather data to demonstrate the ubiquity of peoples or cultures in which government and the state were absent: in other words the widespread occurrence of anarchic polities. I have pointed to limitations of Weber's thesis on the relation between

360

ISBN 1-4120-5679-9

ligence as the major adaptive device for a species. And I am no longer sure that that experiment has been at all successful. We have evolved considerable intelligence, but have used it for the most part quite unintelligently. Certainly no species has been more destructive of this earth or more self destructive. And this destructiveness has increased enormously in the past two centuries. Thus, in the twentieth century there were more deaths from warfare than in all the centuries before. Our environment, to put it conservatively, is threatened. Where are we headed? Is the search in outer space really a part of a program for escape from a destroyed planet earth? Many are today worried about the population explosion, but perhaps within a few generations there won't be any humans around to worry about such a thing. Yet despite all these pessimistic and misanthropic remarks that I have made in this essay, life has been truly a challenging and glorious thing. For where else in this universe have we the pleasant green valleys, the magnificent variety of life, the loving fellowship of which humans are capable? I would like to keep them, but I am not convinced that we will.

Protestantism and capitalism in an article entitled "The Protestant Ethic vs the Spirit of Capitalism?" in the Review of Religious Research.

I have, of course, numerous regrets that have persisted often for long periods - for several decades or more - and nearly all relate to my own either improper or unfair treatment of others. They may appear petty to most readers. But this is the price of being guilt-ridden - of being saddled with that Protestant ethic I have mentioned earlier in this essay.

Before concluding, it has occurred to me that on reading this autobiography readers may suspect that since so much of my time appears to be devoted to travels, that I am a leisured, well heeled "gentleman" which is not the case. Some of my travels were subsidized by grants for research purposes or to go to a place of employment, but a majority were supported by my own finances. Rather than devoting my savings to expensive entertainment and recreation or fashionable clothing, skidoos, and fancy cars I put them into travel.

During the past few years I have come to wonder if I should not re-evaluate my conception of our species and its place in the world. Homo sapiens have been nature's one great experiment in intel-